POWER VS. PERCEPTION:
TEN CHARACTERISTICS OF SELF-EMPOWERMENT FOR WOMEN

POWER VS. PERCEPTION:
TEN CHARACTERISTICS OF SELF-EMPOWERMENT FOR WOMEN

Mary Anne Kochut

A review of some of the challenges "powerful" women encounter on a daily basis as they exert their "power" in either an entrepreneurial venture, climbing the corporate ladder or exercising authority within the course of their daily activities and provides useful tools for self-empowerment to overcome these frustrating challenges.

authorHOUSE®

AuthorHouse™ LLC
1663 Liberty Drive
Bloomington, IN 47403
www.authorhouse.com
Phone: 1-800-839-8640

Published by AuthorHouse   08/15/2013

ISBN: 978-1-4918-0639-5 (sc)
ISBN: 978-1-4918-0638-8 (e)

Library of Congress Control Number: 2013914055

CONTENTS

DEDICATION

To my daughters Vicki and Lori . . . for being the greatest accomplishment of my life; for your love, strength, beauty and faith in me; and my five granddaughters, Jessica, Brianna, Kayla, Annalesse and Alyson . . . for all of you and your own empowerment . . . and I cannot forget to mention the greatest son-in-law ever—Stephen Gleason! I'm so very proud off all of you! Thanks all of you for bringing so much love and joy into my life—in ways that I never imagined were possible!

To Vershelle . . . my mentor and the "big sister" I never had . . . for your inspiration, faith in me, and for seeing my potential when I couldn't see it myself. Thank you for giving me a chance. I know you're singing praises before the "Throne."

. . . And to Sharon; my best friend; you left this world way too soon! I miss you and think of you every day. Thank you for being my friend.

ACKNOWLEDGEMENTS

First and foremost, I am unable to acknowledge anyone or anything without acknowledging that I am only here and able to write this book because of the grace of God in my life, Jesus Christ; who makes all things are possible. Special thanks go to all my friends and clergy (you know who you are) from the various churches and ministries I've been blessed to know or be a part of. Thank you all for all your prayers, inspiration, support; and allowing me to "serve."

I acknowledge my parents and family who instilled in me the importance of faith, character, integrity, a strong work ethic; and taught me I could do anything I want to if I put my mind into it. In addition, I want to acknowledge all my "anonymous" friends who have played an important role in my life, listening to me share my trials, triumphs, joys and tears for over thirty years. We all know where we'd all be without one another.

Also, a big thank you goes to all my former employers; my colleagues, managers and co-workers who supported and inspired me to continue to "push" forward and keep going. I'm blessed and honored to have you as "friends" today.

A special "thanks" goes to Susan RoAne who, along with teaching me *"How to Work a Room,"* approximately twenty years ago; when I expressed my doubts about pursuing a particular life goal because I didn't think I knew enough about the subject, said to me: "You know about as much as the people who are doing it;" which has continued to inspire me over the years to pursue the challenging goals, aspirations and dreams.

I also want to acknowledge Michele Brown who inspired me as my coach and assisted me in clarifying my true goals. Then, there are all those professional and personal relationships that grew into special friendships: Patricia Bershak, Paul Carro, Patrick Diegnan, Kathy Duffy, George Flores, Rev. William H. Halbing, Bill Jensen, Carol Kelly, Bonnie Low-Kramen, Diane Lang, Lee Miller, William M. Monroe, Lucy and Michael Scotti, Lilisa J. Williams, Jeanna Wirtenberg . . . And I can't forget a big "Thank you" to my writing coach—Barry Cohen! All of you have "been there" for me in a very special way. Thank You!

This wouldn't be complete without me acknowledging all of the students who participated in the classes and seminars I've taught over the years. You've all inspired me in more ways than I could ever have taught you.

Last but not least, I feel as if I have to acknowledge the wonderful doctors who first saved my life: Dr. Joanne B.

Kalish, Dr. Andrew S. Greenberg and Dr. Michael J. Kane who treated me from 2001 to 2012, and currently Dr. Paul M. Blum, Dr. Candido E. DeBorja, Jr., Dr. Jennifer A. Wagmiller, Dr. Tobi Greene and Dr. Richard M. Winters who cared for me during the most recent health episode. If it weren't for all of you; your skills, professionalism, knowledge, expertise, and the Grace of God, I wouldn't be here to write this book.

FOREWORD

Mary Anne Kochut captures the essence of power, perseverance and presence in this thoughtful, inspiring and educational book. By generously sharing her own story, Mary Anne gives us a guide to overcoming obstacles. More importantly, she gives us HOPE and a blueprint.

We met two decades ago when we spoke for AT&T at their training center in New Jersey. I was struck by Mary Anne's kindness, warmth and unwavering belief in the importance of building business relationships. How she connected with the participants in our program was matched by how she helped them connect with each other.

Mary Anne understands and has first-hand understanding of the challenges that many women continue to face in the workplace and in life. In this book, she offers practical suggestions and solutions based on her experiences that can be a guideline.

It's several decades later and Mary Anne is still helping others either grow in their current careers or change them.

Her metaphors and analogies make this book engaging, easy to read and interesting.

Whether you're looking for your next career or for an inspirational role model, this book will be your practical partner.

—Susan RoAne, aka The Mingling Maven®, is the author of the classic How To Work a Room® and Face To Face: How To Reclaim The Personal Touch In a Digital World and an international speaker.

ENDORSEMENTS

"Powerful. Empowering. Detailed. Kochut has not only lived a self-empowered life; now this student of life becomes the teacher. She helps us apply common sense lessons in uncommon ways. This is a book for ~~all women~~ all of us. Read it and thrive!"

—Bill Jensen, author of The Courage Within Us and Disrupt! Think Epic. Be Epic.

"Mary Anne Kochut has written a deeply honest and revelatory book for all women. Her advice is profoundly reality-based with every word ringing with truth. In writing this book, Mary Anne has done what she advises to others—give first. It's a new world and we need a new approach which this book clearly provides. Brava!"

—Bonnie Low-Kramen, Bestselling author "Be the Ultimate Assistant"

"Edifying and inspirational message . . . Mary Anne not only "talks the talk," she "walks the walk," by providing a concrete, no-nonsense approach that applies to both professional and personal success. Everyone can benefit from her message!"

—Lee E. Miller, Co-Author, "A Woman's Guide to Successful Negotiating" and "UP: influence Power and the U Perspective-The Art of Getting What You Want"

Mary Anne understands and has first-hand understanding of the challenges that many women continue to face in the workplace and in life. In this book, she offers practical suggestions and solutions based on her experiences that can be a guideline.

—Susan RoAne, aka The Mingling Maven®, is the author of the classic How To Work a Room® and Face To Face: How To Reclaim The Personal Touch In a Digital World and an international speaker.

INTRODUCTION

It's been said that for a woman to be successful she has to work twice as hard as a man. According to Ann M. Morrison, the Glass Ceiling is "not simply a barrier for an individual, based on the person's inability to handle a higher-level job. Rather, it applies to women as a group who are kept from advancing higher because they are women."

Despite the progress that has been made in recent years as women have been moving up the Corporate Ladder, the Glass Ceiling still exists and questions remain regarding women's access to "power" in todays' society and the workplace. If you're really committed to breaking through the glass ceiling, you have to be prepared to wield the hammer.

This book will identify the different types of "power" that exist, some of the challenges that women in leadership roles encounter and provide tools for self-empowerment in dealing with these challenges.

Note: The characteristics, traits and skills discussed in this book are directed towards women who are experiencing every day challenges in the family, community and workplace.

Dysfunctional relationships such as workplace bullying, sexual harassment, domestic violence, addiction, abuse, or any number of special needs that may exist are not addressed. If a woman is the victim of abuse, whether it is workplace bullying, domestic violence, abuse or suffering from an addiction, it's important that she avail herself of the specific resources for those maladies and receive the appropriate therapeutic treatment.

This book can be a recovery tool once the woman is receiving treatment.

PERSONAL STORY

In a book such as this, I think it's important to share my personal story because by applying these characteristics of self-empowerment in some form or another I was able to overcome the many challenges I faced throughout my own life. I learned a real long time ago that "when life gives you lemons you make lemonade" and I was able to face some very difficult times, get through them; and survive and thrive. This hasn't been an easy journey; however, I wouldn't trade one of my "todays" for one of my "yesterdays" because life just keeps getting better and better.

Early Career in Corporate America

Early in my career in corporate America, I was fortunate that I worked for a large corporation where it was ingrained in the culture to support the career development of their employees through internal movement and promotion within the firm. As a result, even though I began my career there with about five years' experience as an administrative assistant at various companies and a high school and a technical school diploma, I was hired in an "entry-level," clerical position. I started as a typist in a typing pool and advanced quickly through several administrative assistant-type roles within the human resource department.

After several years I worked my way "up through the clerical ranks" and was promoted to the managerial levels where I held several individual contributor roles in the training and development department of human resources. In my last role I taught courses on leadership, management, effective communications skills, teambuilding and various professional development skills. I also had the opportunity to travel extensively while delivering these training programs.

This organization provided me with a great career and I loved my job. In addition, I had the opportunity to participate in excellent educational and professional development programs. In these programs I learned many valuable skills, techniques; and an especially increased awareness of human and group dynamics.

Mainly, however, as a result of these professional development opportunities, I came away with an increased awareness of myself and the areas in which I struggled with my own self-development, thought patterns and communications. I learned that in many instances throughout my life and career that there were times when, even though others involved in the situation may have been "wrong," my own behaviors and responses to the situation at hand exacerbated the immediate problems and, at times, made them worse. The result was that I felt like a "victim" in the situation and "rationalized" my own behaviors; whether they were appropriate for the situation or not.

> *"When you develop self-awareness, you will adjust your reactions and gain better control over your situation."*

Growing Up as the "Big Sister"

At this point I think it's important to explain a little more about myself on a personal level. I am the oldest of five children; and I was the only girl; I have four younger brothers. I learned at an early age I was expected to "take care" of others. My father was a violent, abusive alcoholic and the family lived in constant "terror" with the stress of never knowing which one of us would be the next target of his rage. I grew up with the characteristics typical of a child growing up in this type of environment and had no idea how to communicate with another human being.

Learning and education were not rewarded in my family. I was expected to go to school, do my work and stay out of trouble. I made it through school with average grades; I always passed all my subjects—I was "afraid" what would happen to me at home if I didn't. When I was in high school I had the first opportunity to "excel." I was in a school-to-work program in which students from various schools got to compete in subject-related contests regarding the Free Enterprise System of Marketing and Distribution. I didn't want to compete in any of the contests, but I had a good teacher at the time, who saw that I had potential and made it a requirement that I compete in one of the contests. I selected the contest for merchandise display. To my surprise, I "won" first place in my state; which qualified me to go on for National competition where I "won" third place in the Nation.

The fact that I "won" these awards showed me that I that I could be successful. I became interested in education and decided this was the direction I wanted my career to go in. Surely it was obvious that I had the qualifications for a position in this field. As a result I got a part-time assistant position in the display department of a large, local department store. I did well and liked my work. Upon graduation, I applied to various other stores and in each instance I was told that I could not be hired because I was a girl. One manager said, "If you were a 'boy,' I'd hire you in a minute, but I can't hire you because you're a girl." It was the first time I encountered sex discrimination and at the time there was no recourse. I wanted to go to college; however my parents had no money to pay for it so I took a sales associate position with the same department store. I liked it but never really felt like I was reaching my potential; I always felt like I should have been doing something better.

Living "Happily Ever After"—NOT!

The year I turned 20, in an effort to "escape" the situation at home and because I was pregnant, I married a man I had known for about six months. The pregnancy occurred as a result of "date-rape" and, at the time I was so naïve that I didn't even understand what had happened to me . . . until about ten years later when I read an article on date-rape in a women's magazine and realized that was what I had experienced. The man I married was very much like my father; only he wasn't an alcoholic . . . he was a compulsive gambler. However, his behaviors were the same. The only difference was that he did not "drink" or "hit" me. However, the verbal and emotional abuse were no different; nor were the controlling behaviors. I really didn't "love" him, however, I projected a "fairytale-like fantasy" onto him and, from the start he "failed" to live up to my expectations in those fantasies. I was miserable in the marriage from the very beginning. He controlled everything I did and we fought constantly; I literally had gone from the "frying pan and into the fire."

Self-empowerment, although I didn't realize what it was at the time, came to me for the first time during a period when I was experiencing feelings of deep despair and desperation. I felt so helpless, powerless and miserable that for a few seconds, the thought occurred to me that the only way I could "escape" the misery of being under his control of my life was if I was "dead," and maybe I should just "end it all." In what I can only describe as "Divine Intervention," an instant after that thought entered my mind, the next thought was, *"If he can't control me in 'death,' then he can't control me in life!"* I decided to "live" and in that split-second empowered myself to go on.

After that I felt a renewed sense of determination and that I was going to take control of my life . . . even though I had no idea of "how" or what I was going to do.

The news media over the years have been filled with stories of women whose circumstances were similar to mine who chose a "negative" solution to resolve their problems. In my case, however, at that moment, I was able to evaluate the various options that were available to me and, quite frankly, there were quite a few negative solutions that came to mind. However, given the information I had available, at that point in time of my life, I chose the option that served me best. In my case, it was to work . . . and to work hard . . . and that's what I decided to do.

Not long after that, when my daughter was five months old I found a job and started working full-time. I had several jobs; took several months off between the ages of 24 and 25 for maternity leave when I had my second daughter; and worked during the entire 27 years of the marriage.

I'm not going to dwell on any of the specifics of some of the things that occurred in the course of the marriage. For more times than I can count we went to numerous counselors, marriage conferences, etc., with temporary improvement, but ultimately, the situation always reverted back to where it was. So many times people ask me, "Why did you stay?" That's a complicated question and the truth is that in the beginning I was young and naïve . . . I didn't know that I could leave. I didn't know that I had choices, and if a person doesn't know that there are choices, then there is no "choice."

> ***"You always have options. Make the choices***
> ***that support your desired outcomes."***

Later, I realized that I had choices, but after over ten-twenty years, I had two daughters, a house, a mortgage and all bills and debts that go along with it. I felt "trapped" financially and afraid of losing all the material possessions I had accumulated over the years. For years I "rationalized" that I had to accept the situation as it was and try to change what parts of it that I could. I became really good at making up "excuses" for myself and the situation . . . the children; when this one gets married, or when that one graduates, etc., however the "time" was never right.

I had experienced prestige and self-worth through my career advancements and also as an elected official . . . I had run for public office and had won a three-year term on the borough council in the town where I lived. I felt like a hypocrite because professionally and at the public level I was successful and at home I was a victim of mental and emotional abuse.

The best way I can explain it is that I became "comfortable" with the situation and it became my "comfort zone." However, finally there came a time when none of it mattered anymore. Suffice it to say there came a point for me where, the best way to describe it is that I "got sick and tired of being sick and tired," and I started standing up for myself. I had been accepted into a master's degree program to further my education, and finally one day I got an apartment and moved out of the house. The divorce was final approximately one year later. I literally walked away from everything; the house, any property rights, possessions, etc.—all I really had was my job, school, my elected position and a new found sense of freedom and joy.

Finally Free

The first year on my own was great. I was working, my career was progressing, I was having one of the best years of my career; I was exceeding my goals at work, participating in the master's degree program and was exercising the responsibilities of my elected position on the borough council. For the first time in my life I felt a sense of accomplishment and pride. As much as I enjoyed working in the public sector and contributing to the community, I knew that it wasn't a career path that I wanted to pursue. As a result, I chose not to run for re-election for that position so I could focus more on the master's degree program which had become my main priority at the time.

Simultaneously however, drastic and significant changes were occurring in my employer's industry. As a result, the following year, I decided to accept an early retirement "package" to avoid losing my job through downsizing. I really didn't want to leave because I loved what I did. However, I saw that the department was going to be eliminated eventually in this emerging business environment, plus there were significant, lucrative opportunities being offered to me as an independent consultant.

Being in business for myself was a completely different experience for me. I had graduated from the master's program and received my degree; I had some clients and also became an adjunct professor teaching a class at a local university. However, life has a way of "happening" when we have other plans. I went through the loss of my mother and had the opportunity to "forgive" my former husband for the things that happened during the course of our marriage and heal the "rift" between us. I didn't realize how much resentment and anger I was harboring, or how it affected my relationships with my daughters, my attitude and communications in general. The experience was one of "healing" and we were able to have a good relationship after that.

Life Happens

On September 11, 2001, I found out that I had breast cancer had a lumpectomy was treated with chemotherapy, radiation, which took almost a year and then drug therapy for five years. From the very start, I always felt as if it was not a coincidence that I found out I had cancer on 9/11. There's no way of knowing for sure what life has in store for us. However, the people who went to work on that fateful morning thought they'd be going home at the end of the day. One thing that puts things into perspective for me is that I'm still here and unfortunately, many of them are not. I believe I have an obligation to make the most of every day I'm given; that it is a "gift."

I realized through this experience, that there were some things that I might have done differently. I shared some of these thoughts in my story entitled "Choose Your Children's Childhood Over Work" published in Bill Jensen's book, *What is Your Life's Work?* I say, "My career was the most important thing to me. I left my children with babysitters, as there weren't the kind of daycare services available then as there are today. I hardly remember anything about their childhood other than rushing them out of bed in the morning, rushing to the babysitter, rushing to work, picking them up at the end of the day, and then rushing them into bed, and repeating the process the next day.

When they were sick, I couldn't take off of work to stay home with them, so they were bundled up and went to the sitter. I was always busy; never had time for them. I rushed them to grow up and be independent."

I learned that there were some parts of my life where my priorities might have been "mixed up. This experience showed me how easy it is to get distracted by the competing demands of personal and professional life and miss sight of the things that are truly important. I needed to learn to find the balance that would work for me in meeting the daily challenges of personal and professional relationships.

After the treatments I decided that working as an independent consultant was a challenge when going through this type of illness and decided that I should look for another job.

I'm "In Transition . . ." Again??? And Again??? And Again???

At this point it was the summer of 2002 and it was a tough job market. I think that the term, "being in 'transition'" is a way to make people who are out of work feel better about it. In a way, it might be a way to put a more "positive spin" on it, but the fact remains . . . you're still unemployed. It took about two years before I was able to find and accept a temporary position. That "temporary" assignment lasted nine months. After it ended I accepted another "temporary" position which lasted a year. After which I was hired by the same company for the job. In the beginning I was very happy with this position . . . it was my "dream" job. I was an executive with this company and I loved what I did. I had the opportunity to work on managing numerous and diverse projects, as well as developing, designing and delivering training classes on a variety of interesting subjects. I worked for this company for a total of five years, and then in 2010 the position was eliminated due to downsizing.

The job market in 2010 was even worse than it was in 2002 and I was unemployed again. At this point I had over 30 years' experience in my chosen field. I began another job search and went on numerous interviews which always seemed to go "well." When I left the interviews I always felt certain that I "had the job," and it's interesting that I consistently received the same feedback; that another candidate was selected who was a "better fit."

The job-search process can be extremely frustrating; it's a constant, never-ending roller-coaster ride of highs and lows, hope and rejection; and it's critical for anyone who is going through it to stay "positive" at all times. I refused to accept any of the "excuses" my mind would "create" as to "why" and move on to the next potential employer. I volunteered my time to help other people who were also looking for work and kept my skills current by presenting job-search workshops to other people who were unemployed as well as participating in other volunteer activities in the community.

After about a year of continuous job searching, interviews, rejections, etc., something interesting happened; I began to get "calls" from individuals who wanted to "hire" me as their "coach," or I'd get a call from a "client" who would ask me to deliver a training program at their company. The next thing that happened was that I was hired as an adjunct professor to teach at a community college. Work started "showing up."

Then, in January of 2012 I was diagnosed with breast cancer for the second time. I had been cured and was fine for over ten years and this was a complete surprise. It was not a "relapse" of what I had ten years earlier and, even though it was in the same breast, it was a completely different type of cancer. Further testing revealed that I have the BRCA2 gene, which means that the tendency to develop certain types of cancer is hereditary—in both males and females who possess this gene. The treatment for me this time was that I needed to have a mastectomy and chemotherapy.

During the entire time I was still looking for a job, going on interviews and teaching my class at the community college; in fact, I was back in my classroom teaching one week post-op and I even taught a couple of classes for one of my clients. Approximately three weeks after I completed the chemotherapy I was asked to speak at a businesswomen's group on self-empowerment. My presentation was extremely well received by the women at this group. Not long after that I was invited to speak on the same subject at two other women's leadership conferences and in both instances the participants found my presentations extremely enlightening and applicable to their businesses, careers and lives. At this writing I have undergone four surgeries within a little more than a year's time. I had a second mastectomy, purely as a precautionary measure because of the BRCA2 condition, and the beginning of the reconstruction process. I have completed three quarters of the reconstruction process and at this point I am facing the final steps. I am cancer free and feel great.

> *"I was trying to recreate my comfort zone
> and missing the unlimited possibilities that
> are available."*

When I was going through the chemotherapy treatments this second time, something that I can't explain "happened" to me; all I can say is that I woke up "different" one morning and my situation took on a completely different focus. I suddenly "saw" everything, life, business, career—differently. I realized that by trying to find another job I was trying to re-create my comfort zone and that I was missing unlimited possibilities. I concluded that the best way for me to have the perfect job would be for me to create it myself. So, instead of looking for a job in another company that would be a right "fit" for me, I decided to empower myself by forming my own company; thereby, creating my own job which is a perfect "fit" for me. I felt a strong "passion," desire and drive to share these concepts that I applied throughout my life, career and fighting cancer, to empower other women in the ways in which I have learned to "empower" myself;

and this book is the result. Combined with my faith, the characteristics and tools presented in this book are what carried me through these experiences in my life. They are not easy to apply; however, whenever I am faced with the next challenge, the question I ask myself is: "Is there anything I can do about this right now, this minute?" If the "answer" is "yes," then I "do it." If the answer is "no," then I tell myself I have to "accept" it, move on and find something that I can "do" something about. In a nutshell . . . that is self-empowerment. However, it's not always an easy thing to do. My hope is that my experiences will inspire you to do the work that you need to do for your own self-empowerment to become "unstoppable" in living your dreams!

Mary Anne Kochut

CHAPTER 1

Position Power vs. Personal Power

Position Power vs Personal Power	
Position Power	**Personal Power**
• Power bestowed by institution	• Comes from within self
• Level	• Persuasive
• Protocol	• Respect
• Supported by policy	• Charisma
• Sanctioned	• Type of person you are
• Authority	• Knowledge
	• Experience
	• Connections/Network

Typically women have not been acculturated to manage "power" well. Traditionally they have been trained by various societies to be the caregivers, nurturers and to provide "support" to the people in "power" positions.

In her groundbreaking book, *Games Mother Never Taught You: Corporate Gamesmanship for Women,* Betty Jean Harragan begins by stating, "Working is a game women never learned to play." In describing some of the typical problems women encounter in the workplace, she goes on to say, these women . . ."are exceedingly accomplished working women who are suffering from traumatic experiences in their jobs. Their problems are having a disproportionate impact on their life plans, their feelings, and their future employment. Their situations are typical." She goes on to say she hears almost the same story continuously from "equally competent, ambitious women." She then continues, "What their mothers, teachers, husbands, friends and employers have taught them—deliberately or unwittingly—has managed to distort their perspective, warp their judgment, pervert their trust, exploit their goodwill, distract their common sense and divert their energy to helping everyone but themselves."

Betty explains that the game of business is the existing system. "The landscape which has been contoured out of a military-sports subsoil is the territory of play, the game board. The rules of the game are those firmly established generations ago . . . ." She explains further that, ". . . anyone who wants to join in the game must, perforce subscribe to the standard rules of play. It does not follow that all players who meekly accede to the rules will win." She also says that it's important for women not to get deflected, distracted or discouraged simply because they don't know the ground rules of what is strictly a "boys' game."

The old saying is, "Behind every great man there's a great woman;" but what about these great women when it comes to power and exercising authority? A plethora of negative stereotypes are assigned to these women by society throughout the ages from the "evil stepmother" of Cinderella fame up to Meryl Streep as Miranda Priestly of "The Devil Wears Prada" movie. However, before discussing these stereotypes it's important to understand a little more about "power."

What Do We Mean by "Power?"

The early scene from the movie "The Devil Wears Prada" where Miranda arrives at the office comically addresses the issue of how the use of "power" can impact the entire culture of an organization. Everyone was "walking on eggshells" and attempting to avoid who would be the "target of her wrath" that morning. While this is a Hollywood movie, it does demonstrate how one person's use of their "power" can impact an organization.

The first thing that needs to be explored is what is meant by "power" and authority. There are two types of power that is exercised in society, whether in the corporate world, government, academia or the family. They are: Position Power and Personal Power.

Position Power is bestowed by the institution. It is indicated by level, or title, i.e., president, vice president, director, manager, supervisor, police officer, professor, teacher, mother, etc. These titles command certain protocols and are supported by policies, sanctions and authority within the systems of the institution—whether it's a large corporation, the military, government agency, educational institution or family.

Personal Power is given by others. It comes from within the individual; in the way he or she attempts to influence or persuade others to accomplish tasks and the respect he or she conveys towards other people. It's based on an aura of "charisma," their personality or the type of person they are; as well as their knowledge, experience and connections. We know what this is when we experience it in our interactions with other people, i.e., "that doctor has a nice 'bedside manner,'" "that salesperson has a 'bad attitude,'" etc.

One kind of power is not better than the other and everyone has both kinds of power. The challenge is that some people are more comfortable with one kind of power than the other. This has nothing to do with gender but is more related to the individual person's comfort zone. What happens is that the individual exhibits behaviors based on the type of power they are most comfortable with. This is fine in situations where those behaviors are appropriate for the situation. It can create problems, however, when the situation calls for behaviors that are from the least-comfortable form of power; and that is where problems can arise.

In the book *The Promotable Woman,* Norma Carr-Ruffino, Ph.D. states that, "Women are much more likely than men to use leadership power based on charisma, work record and contacts," (personal power), "rather than organizational position power. They rarely use coercion, while men's use of power is more likely to be coercive. Women are more interested in empowering others." She says that women have a more inclusive style, are more willing to deal with employees as equals and include them in their "inner circle." They rarely or never give orders and prefer to include employees in the decision-making process. She goes on to say, "Women don't see their position in the organization as a platform for influence. Instead, they operate from their personal base of influence, their relationships with employees, and their expertise with the work," (personal power).

Jane's Story

For example: Jane is a manager who is most comfortable with communicating through the use of her personal power. She manages a team of project managers. She "likes" the members of her team and they "like" her as well. She had been assigned a very high priority project. When she delegated the work assignments to her team members she said she would "like" it if everyone submitted their work by the deadline.

She became very frustrated when none of her staff members submitted their work on time. When she spoke to them about it she learned that her staff members didn't understand the level of priority of the missed deadlines because she said she "would 'like' it," and didn't realize the level of priority the project held: that it was critical to the success of the project that the deadlines be met.

A caution here; sometimes a person in a situation such as Jane's will "swing" the pendulum to the other extreme and "react" as a way to "lay down the law;" "read them the 'riot' act," etc. While it might provide a temporary solution, the long-term effects are that these types of behaviors typically backfire and create additional managerial, supervisory and interpersonal problems from which some of the negative stereotypes listed in the next chapter are based.

While Jane "expected" her staff would submit their work on time because they share a mutual good rapport, she needed to learn to become more comfortable with exerting her position power when necessary. She needed to communicate more effectively and clearly the work priorities to her team members and institute consequences when deadlines were not met in a manner that was appropriate to their organizational culture and policies.

For example, in a military environment, drill sergeants give "orders" based upon their position and the team members follow those orders . . . They say "jump" and the team "jumps." It's very clear, necessary and appropriate for that culture and environment.

However, most organizations in the private sector have a more open and participative culture and Jane needs to learn new skills and behaviors that are appropriate in that environment.

The key is balance: Balancing position and personal power. It means drawing upon the appropriate "power" for the situation at hand and being able to recognize or "diagnose" the situation and which way is best to respond. For women, when "power" is used inappropriately, the danger of being "stereotyped" occurs. The next chapter briefly lists some common stereotypes women encounter in society.

CHAPTER 2

Negative Stereotypes about Powerful Women

Perception vs. Reality

We've all heard the old saying: "perception is reality." That can be true for the person doing the "perceiving," however, it may not be "true" for the person being "perceived;" and this is where dangerous "stereotyping" occurs. Typically these "stereotypes" or "perceptions" are wrong and that's especially true for women in positions of "power." Unfair and damaging "stereotypes" are projected onto women more so than their male counterparts.

Valerie Young, Ed.D., author of *The Secret Thoughts of Successful* Women says, "Women face harsh, limiting assessments based on their gender. Women are being judged more, even by other women. "While male leaders are allowed to have complex personalities, powerful women are often summed up by hackneyed stereotypes that undermine them and their power."

In her March 6, 2013 article entitled, *"Beware of Broken Glass: The Media's Double Standard for Women at the Top"* for *The Verge*, Elizabeth Spiers describes how the press attacked Sheryl Sandberg, COO of Facebook and Marissa Mayer, CEO of Yahoo, for being strong, ambitious leaders and instituting change within their organizations. Unlike their male counterparts these women were mercilessly "attacked" for the tough business decisions and policies they made for the success of their companies.

Jenna Goudreau wrote an article in the October 2011 edition of *Forbes* Magazine that identified ten of the Worst Stereotypes about Powerful Women.

They are listed here for informational purposes only.

1. Ice Queen	6. Conniving
2. Single and Lonely	7. Emotional
3. Tough	8. Angry
4. Weak	9. Token
5. Masculine	10. Cheerleader

The purpose of this book is to provide tools for self-empowerment and dwelling on these stereotypes would be counter-productive. However, there's no doubt that they exist and that women are encountering them every day. They will be referred to throughout the text where appropriate. Women need to be aware that any one or several of these stereotypes can be projected on to them from members of society . . . both male and female.

Misunderstandings, Miscommunications or Differences in Work Styles

These types of stereotypes can be created as a result of misunderstandings, miscommunications or differences in work styles, especially between men and women. In addition to this, while I'm not *blaming the victim*, so-to-speak, women need to understand where and how their own behaviors might be contributing to the perceptions that bring on this type of negative stereotyping. For example, I remember some of my former female colleagues who, upon returning to the workplace after having their children, tended to act "apologetic" for the time they took off to have and care for their children. As a result they came across as lacking confidence and having low self-esteem. This can contribute to the *weak* and/or *emotional* stereotypes. I also remembering hearing some of my former female colleagues making jokes about having *Mommy Brain*, which can contribute to the *cheerleader* or *token* stereotypes. Women need to project a sense of confidence and pride of their role as a mother and not apologize for their life decisions. On the other hand, I've seen men return from paternity leave and get right back to work . . . no apologies, no excuses etc.

Diane Lang, MA, who wrote the book, *Baby Steps: The Path from Motherhood to Career,* said that the greatest driver of a woman's success is "Different for every woman." From what she's seen and worked with the greatest factor is "A woman's need for personal and professional accomplishment and to be a role model for her kids."

One of the greatest challenges women have faced in the past, she goes on to say, is "themselves. It's the limiting beliefs that they aren't good enough or that they can't do it. It's basically fear. She said that the challenges are the same today, "But also for women who are in mid-life, it's figuring out what they want. They no longer want the career they had before kids and their values have changed. They want a job that has more purpose and passion in life."

She says that women who are encountering the effects of stereotyping early in their careers need to "Prove they are wrong! Be the best employee, supervisor you could be! If you hit the glass ceiling, find another way or start your own niche/biz! Never give up."

In her book, *The Promotable Woman,* Norma Carr-Ruffino, Ph.D., created a comparison of male and female managers utilizing the work of Sally Helgesen from her book, *The Female Advantage: Women's Ways of Leadership,* and Henry Mintzberg from his book *The Nature of Managerial Work.* The results of her comparison are illustrated in the following table.

| Comparison of Male and Female Managers ||
Mintzberg's stude of male managers	Helgesen's study of female managers
Men worked at an unrelenting pace, with no breaks in activity during the day	Women worked at a steady pace, with small breaks
Men's days were characterized by interruptions, discontinuity, and fragmentation.	Women viewed unscheduled tasks and encounters as a chance to be accessible to team members, to be involved, responsible, caring and helpful.
Men showed a preference for live action encounters.	Women preferred live action encounters, but scheduled time to attend to mail.
Men lacked time for reflection.	Women focused on the ecology of leadership, finding time for reflection and keeping the long term in focus, relating decisions to their larger effect upon families, education, environment, even world peace.
Men maintained a complex network of relationships with people outside the organization.	Women maintained a complex network of relationships with people outside the organization.
Men identified themselves with their jobs.	Women identified themselves as complex and multifaceted.
Men had difficulty sharing information	Women scheduled time for sharing information

The Promotable Woman, Norma Carr-Ruffino, Ph.D.

**"Empowerment comes from knowing the
truth about yourself and not allowing the
perceptions of others to influence you."**

For example, based on the first example in the table, where it indicates that men prefer to work at an unrelenting pace without taking breaks, a male manager may perceive that when a female co-worker or employee takes periodic short breaks that she is not "working" as hard as she should be, or possibly, not taking her work seriously enough, or any number of negative stereotypes that he can make up just as a result of a difference in perception of their preferred work styles.

The key to dealing with situations such as this is to recognize them and not react to them. The reality is that, in life there will be people who will "like" you and people who won't; people who share your preferences and people who won't; people who work the same way you do and people whose work style is different from yours. If you react to the negativity, you run the "danger" of becoming a "self-fulfilling prophesy:" which is exactly what your opponents want. Communicate effectively. Be yourself. Do your job. Be authentic. Empowerment comes from knowing the "truth" about yourself and not allowing the perceptions of others to influence you. Not an easy thing to do; however, necessary for self-empowerment and becoming a leader, whether that is in the workplace, the community or the family. The following chapters provide some useful tools for learning how to "respond" and not "react" when dealing with these types of situations.

My Experiences With Stereotyping

Several examples from my own experience with stereotyping follow. The first occurred early in my career

13

shortly after I had been promoted into my first role as a corporate trainer for a large, global organization. The manager who promoted me into the position was an excellent "people manager" who was great at providing feedback and coaching. What I didn't realize then, however, was that I was experiencing the effects of two negative stereotypes: "weak" and "emotional" and these two stereotypes were manifested both individually and "intermingled" with one another. Also, I was unaware at the time that some of my own behaviors perpetuated the stereotype.

To provide some background, when I was promoted into this position I had a great deal of background in the area of design, development and evaluation of training but practically no experience teaching. I was highly motivated and excited about the job but needed a great deal of coaching and professional development; which I mainly received "in the classroom" by observing and co-instructing with other trainers. I didn't receive any "formal" training on delivering training classes. Needless to say, in the beginning when I was just starting out in the role, oftentimes many of the evaluations I received from the students in my classes were "less than 'glowing;'" which "bothered" me.

As a consequence, when discussing the overall results of these early evaluations with my manager, I would become "defensive" and place "blame" on others and engage in "victim-type" behaviors, such as complaining, etc. I also expressed that I often felt "overwhelmed" with all the projects I was working on and worried about getting all my projects completed on time. He was a good listener and coach and typically would allow me to "vent" and then steer me towards things I could do to improve these results; sometimes moving some projects around, rescheduling others, etc. However, I was always able to juggle all of the priorities and get the projects completed on time. My thoughts, however, are that this is where the "emotional" and "weak" stereotypes occurred because, while I wasn't aware of it at the time, I believe he became "over-protective" of me in an attempt to be "spared" or avoid more of my "venting" episodes.

Here is one example of how this played out at work. There was an occasion early in my role when I was assigned to teach a class outside of the headquarters location in a field location. In this field location the corporate culture was different from the headquarters "culture" that I was used to. The participants were skilled craft-workers who worked in the factories and outdoors; and they had a reputation for being "rough and tough." My manager was concerned that I would not be able to "handle" these employees and, although I was not concerned about working with them, he made arrangements for another male trainer to co-instruct the class with me and he also sat in on the class himself to observe "our" performance.

What was interesting is that I had no problems teaching the class or managing these employees; they were great students and I received excellent evaluations from them. I proved to my manager that his concern was unwarranted and I could manage myself and didn't need to be "protected."

Another way in which these two stereotypes were manifested with this manager, however, is that I was not assigned to high-profile projects within the organization that would have provided me with higher-level exposure. This had a negative impact on my career development. For example, the organization was involved in a high-level, corporate-wide, culture-changing training initiative for which many of the other trainers were being certified; however, I was not. At this point I had been in the role for a few years. When I requested to be included in the certification my manager told me that he didn't think I was "ready" to teach this particular program because of the controversial nature of the content. I was disappointed; however, he was "firm" in his decision and I was unable to convince him otherwise. I continued to request his approval and, finally, after two years I was certified in the program. As in the past, I did very well and received excellent evaluations for the program. My manager later "apologized" to me for making me wait so long for the certification and told me that he appreciated my "persistence" in obtaining his approval for the certification.

After approximately five years, a corporate re-organization took place and I was assigned to another manager: a woman. Her "style" was very different from my previous manager. She was extremely goal oriented and results driven and I believe that the "tough" stereotype was unfairly assigned to her. However, I never noticed any "protective" behaviors that I was "used to" and comfortable with from my previous manager, and after a couple of communications "miss-fires" I learned to work very well with her. In fact, I have to say that she was the "best" manager I ever had. Here's why:

Shortly before she became my manager, I was in the process of applying to a master's degree program at a major university. In one of our conversations I shared with her that I was feeling overwhelmed with all the work and was starting to have second thoughts about applying for this advanced degree. I expected her to "agree" with me (as my previous manager usually did) and was getting ready to just "give up." To my surprise, she didn't do that! What she did was encourage me to continue with the application process and not to "give up." She inspired me to "stay-the-course" and if it hadn't been for her I would never have been accepted into the program or have received the master's degree.

> *"True leadership involves encouraging others to empower themselves to overcome their challenges."*

I am forever grateful to her. She demonstrated true leadership by encouraging me, as her employee, to empower myself to overcome the challenges I was facing at that time. She saw through my struggles and identified my potential and "coached" me through them, however, she didn't make it "easier" for me. She then provided me with the inspiration and motivation to overcome the obstacles and challenges that were stopping me from pursuing my dream of receiving this advanced degree.

As demonstrated by this manager, the next step towards self-empowerment is to understand what is meant by leadership; from a personal perspective, which means how one "leads" his or her life as well as those individuals who are functioning in leadership roles, such as the manager described previously. The next chapter explores some of the common theories and presents some useful tools for effective leadership.

CHAPTER 3

Leadership Principles

These leadership principles apply to both males and females; however, the reality is that since women in leadership positions are relatively new to leadership roles within the workforce, the challenges they face can be greater.

As a result, for a woman to be effective in a leadership role she needs to adapt these characteristics and skills even more so than her male counterparts.

Leadership: There are various theories regarding leadership. Below are some quotations:

What is Leadership?

"The ability to get others to do what they don't want to do and like it. "   Harry S. Truman

"Getting people to do what they really don't want to do and don't feel equipped to do against a timeline they don't believe in with risks that scare them to achieve an objective they believe at the beginning is impossible."   Eric Gregory

"If you think you are a leader and you look behind and nobody is following you... you are not a leader."   Gandhi

Dr. Stephen Covey, who was an expert on leadership and wrote the award-winning book, *The Seven Habits of Highly Effective People,* did a study in 1976 for his doctoral dissertation. In this study he wanted to identify what constituted success in the United States for the first 200 years of its history. He called this his "Bicentennial Study."

What he found was that, prior to World War I, the success literature that he reviewed he described as being "character based." What it showed was that the characteristics that produced eventual success for a person or organization were thought to be basic character traits, or values; things like honesty, integrity, industry, thrift, charity, service, etc. The content of Benjamin Franklin's autobiography is a good example of the essence of this type of literature.

Then he noticed a shift occurred during the next fifty years; which has manifested in today's society about what the fundamental assumptions are relating to personal and interpersonal success. This new focus targeted personality development as the key to success instead of character development. A person's external behaviors were considered more important than his or her internal character traits. The emphasis was placed on behavioral techniques of how-to's, what a person "did," body language and various other processes of human interactions . . . or a person's personality as opposed to his or her character. The end result of this became a mindset that focused on how to get what you want. This then promoted an orientation toward manipulation and a quick-fix. For instance, the idea of service and relationship development was abandoned in sales training and manipulative selling tactics took its place.

Dr. Covey relates this shift in the leadership development mindset to an iceberg. The base of the iceberg represents what the person stands for, or his or her "character" underneath the surface of the water; or what can't be seen; their values, integrity and vision, which comprises his or her character.

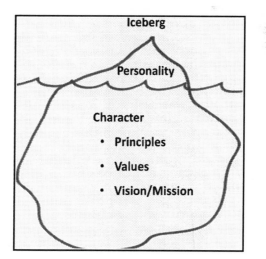

The top or the tip of the iceberg which can be seen above the water line is what people "see;" the personality; their mannerisms, physical appearance, (are they "attractive?"), how they "smile," make eye contact, shakes hands, dress, etc. These are the things that can be learned about an individual in a matter of minutes; they are visible to the naked eye.

Who's Following Who?

Leadership constitutes what makes up the greatest mass of the iceberg; what lies beneath the water line; the character, the principles, the vision and mission. This represents the things that people cannot "see" but rather, have to be learned over time. Relationships develop over time. Effective leaders are consistent over time and build relationships with others based on integrity, honesty, trust, etc.

The key to leadership is not what can be "seen" in a person, but rather is based upon his or her character; which is the base of the iceberg. It is what that person stands for; what is known about him or her, his or her reputation; how he or she manages crisis situations, how they respond to and communicate with others.

Leadership is about who would follow that person. Ghandi said: "If you think you're a leader and you look around and there's no one following you; you're not a leader." A leader is defined by the people who follow them. While technical expertise, experience and organizational knowledge are important, the greater portion of this is based upon their "personal" power; the kind of example they set and how they interact, communicate and treat the people they lead.

Successful Leaders

For leaders to be successful, they need to approach and live their role from the "base" of the iceberg; from the basis of their personal character; their principles, values and commitment to the vision or mission of their role. If a leader exhibits basic character traits in his or her interactions and communications with others, things like personal integrity, being trustworthy, truthful, honest, etc., then he or she is demonstrating the basic traits of an effective leader . . . or leadership.

For leaders to be truly self-empowered, their behavior needs to be consistent over time. While this is an important skill for men to master as well, it's critical for women because of the negative stereotypes that are more freely assigned to them. They need to develop resiliency to recover from the continuous "hits" brought on by continuous changes. For example continuing to "trust" people after experiencing a betrayal of a trusted employee, or business associate, continuing to be a "risk-taker" after a "calculated risk" has gone awry. Self-empowerment comes from developing the resiliency to bounce back from these kinds of setbacks and survive and thrive in a world of continuous change. They need to "step out" of their "comfort zone" and manage the continuous changes that are happening on a daily basis. This "comfort zone" consists of the habitual behaviors that they have established over time that dis-empower them and can lead to ineffective leadership behaviors and misuse of power. Self-empowered leaders need to identify what these behaviors and mindsets are that are sabotaging their effectiveness and replace them with new ones that foster self-empowerment.

Would a Man be "Judged" as Harshly?

A good example of this is described in "The Daily Beast," article on March 8, 2013, regarding, Facebook's COO Sheryl Sandberg, (discussed earlier), who defended Yahoo's CEO Marissa Mayer from the criticisms she'd been receiving regarding the business decisions she made and instituted in her organization. Sandberg says that Mayer would not be judged so harshly if she were a man. Both Sandberg and Mayer are focusing on the business needs and are not reacting negatively to their critics and set a great example for self-empowerment for themselves and one another.

The Ten Characteristics for Self-Empowerment described in the following chapters are particularly important for women to master because of the added pressures imposed on them by societal perceptions. These characteristics of self-empowerment are designed to help leaders develop resiliency for work/life balance and effectiveness; whether in a business environment, performing community/ charitable work or in their personal lives.

CHAPTER 4

Resiliency: The Ten Characteristics of Self-Empowerment

Introduction to Resiliency Model: Much of the work that has been done on Change Management in recent years is rooted in the Kurt Lewin theory of "un-freeze, change, and freeze." What this means is that a "system" (or an individual) is "frozen" into its processes, (habits), etc. When the time comes to institute a "change," the system is then "unfrozen" and the change (new process/behavior) is instituted; then the "system" is then "frozen" into place again. This theory worked well into the middle of the 20th Century. However, towards the end and into the Technology Age of the 21st Century this theory doesn't work as well because it assumes that the new "change" will have a chance to "freeze" into place again. With the speed of technology, communications and Globalization, multiple changes are occurring simultaneously and a system doesn't get the chance to "freeze" into the new process(es). However, organizations and leaders are continuing to operate out of the original mindset.

Continuous Change

Developing "resiliency" from the multiple impacts of these multiple changes occurring simultaneously is a key element in self-empowerment. It is important for both men and women; however, it is even more critical for women because women are judged more harshly based upon the stereotypes listed in Chapter 2. The Ten Characteristics of Self-Empowerment are built into the Resiliency Leadership Model. It can apply to one's business or personal life.

What does "resiliency" mean? According to Merriam-Webster resiliency is:

1. The capability of a strained body to recover its size and shape after deformation caused especially by compressive stress.
2. An ability to recover from or adjust easily to misfortune or change."

Both of these definitions can apply to resiliency. As women we need to look at how we recover from the "compressive stress" of continuous changes we experience in both our professional and personal lives. What kind of strain does it apply to our bodies? How do we handle stress? What happens to our disposition and our attitude when plans have to change or unexpected events or emergencies occur? How do we adjust to and deal with the changes that occur in daily life?

Compressive Stress!

For example, Linda is a single mother of three boys; eight, six and three years old. She is a high performer, does excellent work, always manages to get all her work completed, meets or "beats" her deadlines, is a team player and gets along well with her colleagues and team members. Her boss understands her situation to a certain extent and allows her the flexibility to work from home when necessary.

Linda struggles every day with child care issues, work issues and the activities involved in everyday life. It's stressful enough coordinating all the activities when everything goes according to the "planned schedule;" however, if one of the children becomes sick or there's a problem with the child-care provider and she needs to leave work, it creates problems on her job. This happens on a regular basis and means Linda has the added stress of having to care for a sick child plus the additional pressures that are occurring during her absence at work. For example, meetings need to be rescheduled; deadlines need to be re-negotiated, colleagues and team members have to "pitch" in and "cover" projects in her absence, etc.

Recently, however, despite her excellent work record, Linda has received feedback that she's "perceived" as being "overly emotional" by senior leadership in the organization. To counteract this negative stereotype, Linda needs to learn how to manage the changes that are occurring in her personal life in a way that empowers her and does not lend itself towards the behaviors that are associated with the "emotional" stereotype.

For Linda, the changes occurring in daily her life are usually of a negative nature; however, it really doesn't matter whether the change is a positive or negative; the stress is the same. The body cannot distinguish between the two, which is why mastering these Ten Characteristics of Self-Empowerment are critical.

CHAPTER 5

Resiliency Hourglass Model

Because of the multiple "hats" that must be worn in the workplace, family, etc., women, like Linda, are expected to be able to "do" and "have" it "all" and multitasking is a critical skill for anyone to master in the 21st Century. For women, the necessity is multiplied. As I myself had to learn, developing the resiliency to recover from the constant "hits" coming in from all directions related to all of these roles is the critical component needed to survive and thrive in this constantly changing environment.

Hourglass Definition: To present the model, I created a metaphor of an hourglass. An hourglass is defined as an instrument for measuring time consisting of a glass vessel having two compartments from the uppermost of which a quantity of sand runs into the lower one in an hour.

I chose an hourglass as the representative of the model for several reasons:

1. An hourglass can only do its job as a result of constant change because;
2. The sand inside is always being shaken up, as the hourglass itself has to be turned upside down in order for it to function.

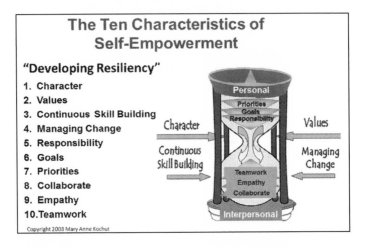

Resiliency Hourglass: Each part of the model represents a particular characteristic and the associated behaviors or needed skills related to it. The two parts of the inner hourglass consist of a vessel that is held together by an outer frame. Without this frame, the hourglass would not function because the glass would not stand upright and would fall apart.

CHAPTER 6

Characteristics 1 and 2— Character and Values

Pillars

Character and Values: Four columns, which act as the "pillars" for leadership, connect the top portion to the bottom portion of the hourglass. The two in the back that are not completely visible, represent personal character and values; which corresponds to the "base" of the "iceberg" mentioned previously and is the foundation for leadership. Character is a person's spirituality; personal integrity, honesty, work ethic, etc. Values are his or her personal values, ethics and spiritual beliefs. Our personal values are what influence how we make decisions. I truly believe that it was the influence of these two characteristics that prompted my first positive choice towards self-empowerment that is described in my personal story at the beginning of this book.

These two characteristics work together and, based upon them, is what creates a person's interests, inner drives, or his or her inner "passions" in life; what is truly in his or her "heart." This is illustrated by the "Heart Model" described as follows:

Passion: What's Flowing from the "Heart"

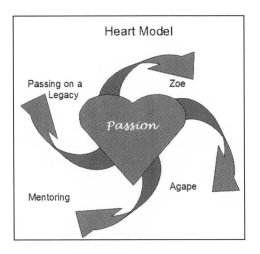

Heart Model: Values flow from a person's "heart" and combine to create his or her "passion;" which can be compared to a "burning fire" within. The four drives indicated in the "Heart Model" flow from that passion.

Zoe:	Comes from the Greek, which means life, or to live. It is the quality of living our life. Are we happy? Do we experience a sense of joy and satisfaction in our daily life?
Agape:	Also comes from the Greek, which means to love unconditionally. It is the quality of our relationships with our spouse, family, friends, etc.
Mentoring:	We are open to learning and sharing our knowledge with others. We are willing to show others the "ropes," so-to-speak and help more-junior people along the way.
Passing on a Legacy:	How do we want to be remembered after we leave this world? What are we going to "pass on" to the next generation?

Self-empowerment begins when we identify and understand what our own "drives" are within us and this is one of the foundational elements of self-empowerment and self-satisfaction.

For example, Linda is passionate about her life. She loves her family and her work (Zoe). She is a loving mother who is committed to instilling her values and ethics into the lives of her children (Agape). She is a "giving" person and genuinely cares about the people she works with. She shares her expertise and knowledge with her colleagues because she truly wants them to excel and progress in their careers as well (Mentoring). Linda's passion for her work and her family and sharing her expertise, values and ethics with her family and colleagues is the result of all these elements operating simultaneously (Passing on a Legacy). It is what drives her behavior and gives meaning and satisfaction to her life.

Everyone possesses all of these drives. Self-empowerment begins when we create our own sense of mission or purpose by identifying what these internal drives consist of for us; and then focus our energy and our actions on living our life around them.

Personal character and values are the foundational piece of self-empowerment because they help us to understand what is truly important in our lives and we can focus our activities around the things that contribute most to them.

CHAPTER 7

Characteristics 3 and 4—Continuous Skill Building and Managing Change

Continuous Skill Building and Managing Change: Columns three and four, Continuous Skill Building and Managing Change work together hand-in-hand. Typically when change occurs, one needs to learn new skills in order to adjust and adapt to the change.

Early in my career as a corporate trainer, the only visual training aids that were available at the time were overhead transparencies, easel charts, dry erase "white boards" and VHS video. My colleagues and I would spend hours creating and re-creating the same "pre-boards" on easel pads for use in our classrooms. It was a time-consuming process.

Around the time I left that organization, presentation software entered upon the scene and I had to learn how to develop presentations via this software. It was an incredible timesaving device. I only had to create a presentation once and I could use it over and over again for the same class. No more spending hours writing out the material on easel charts.

Imagine where I would be in today's world if I was unable to embrace the change in technology and be open to the characteristic of "Continuous Skill Building."

Learning New Ways of Doing Things

Continuous Skill Building: This means that we have to always be open to learning new ways of thinking and doing things. As I had to learn new skills to utilize the new PowerPoint technology in the classroom, we may have to develop our skills in any given area, either physically, emotionally, socially or spiritually. It may become necessary for us to get additional training, go back to school and get additional degrees or certifications or learn new technologies just so that we can perform our jobs. If we don't we will be left behind as technology advances and changes how people communicate and move forward, which is why the next characteristic, Managing Change, is critical to developing resiliency and self-empowerment. For example, Linda had a habit of openly sharing with her colleagues, team members, internal clients or anyone who would listen, the many problems she was having with her children regarding their illnesses, schools, transportation, visitation, custody, child care and general family issues. She wasn't aware of it, but, as a result, she began to get a "reputation" as a "complainer," hence, the "perception" of being "overly emotional."

Linda needed to learn to employ more effective coping mechanisms to deal with the continuous stressors of her parenting and family life. Not to minimize the severity of the problems she was experiencing, she needed to exercise prudence with whom she shared her problems with and develop a support network. She was able to accomplish this by privately confiding in only one or two trusted colleagues who would not participate in the "office rumor mill" and perpetuate the negative perception. She also joined a parenting support group which provided her with the outlet she needed to "vent" her frustrations in an appropriate, safe environment where she received useful feedback and support. She was provided resources that gave her the support she needed to manage the family issues and problems she was experiencing which were creating the negative "perception" of being "overly emotional."

Learning new skills and behaviors is not always an easy thing to do. Change is not easy, but as Linda discovered, once we break through and get to the other side, it's well worth it, which is why "Managing Change" is the fourth characteristic.

Getting Out of the "Comfort Zone . . . 'But I like it here!'"

Managing Change: As human beings we do not like change. We like to create and remain in our "comfort zone" and can also think that the needs of our job will always remain the same.

There's one conversation I remember having with my daughter not long after she started her first job. She had recently graduated high school and accepted a clerical support role as a receptionist for a local manufacturing firm. She had said that she thought she'd always have a job because companies always needed "someone to answer the phone." This was in the days before voicemail was universally in use, and, it goes without saying, she was in for a big surprise. Imagine any company today without a mechanized phone system.

We need to prepare ourselves for the changes that are being imposed by changing technologies and recognize that, depending on the extent of the changes, it may not necessarily be an easy transition.

Five Stages of Grieving: Elizabeth Kubler-Ross identified the Five Stages of Grieving; in her book *On Death and Dying,* which she wrote after working with people who had been advised that they had been diagnosed with a fatal disease. These stages are: denial, anger, bargaining or negotiating, depression and then acceptance; they do not necessarily occur in this order and an individual can "bounce" around among several of them before they get to the last stage of "acceptance." These "stages" also occur when an individual experiences "change."

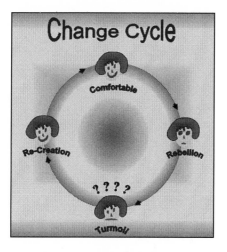

Change Cycle: We all go through a change cycle whenever we experience any kind of change. First, we are comfortable with the way things are, we do not believe that the change will really happen; we've got our "plans" and things are going to go according to "our plan." This is the "denial" stage and is demonstrated by our first reaction when we hear that something happened . . . we say something like: "Oh no!" or "Not again!" or "Oh no, you did not!" or "Don't tell me that!" or something along those lines. The point is that we immediately "deny" the news we have just received.

There's "No Way" I'm Doing That!

Then we hear that the change is really coming and we go into rebellion, thus the "anger" stage. We resist; we've got "our plan!" We get angry and frustrated. Some people may "yell," others become "silent," depending on how they handle anger. They may "blame" other people, special circumstances, make excuses, or have various reactions as they go into turmoil. The point is that we are confused or maybe feel "torn." We don't know what to do. We cannot handle it. Here we may be in the "bargaining/negotiating stage; we think things like: "If I had done 'this,' then 'that' wouldn't have happened," or, "if only 'this' had happened." When we finally figure out that none of the "if onlys" and "shoulda, woulda, coulda's" don't work . . . then the depression" stage "hits" because we cannot change anything; the change is still happening.

However, as the change happens, we start to get used to doing things the "new" way. As we get into it, and "practice" the new way of doing things, it becomes easier; it is not as bad as we thought it would be and we begin to get used to it. We go to the re-creation stage of the cycle or "acceptance," and then become comfortable again and start the "cycle" over. Our "comfort zone" is the stage in which we are "comfortable."

When learning new skills it might become uncomfortable to grasp them right away. The key is to stick with it and practice until it becomes comfortable. The goal is to get to the point where it is second nature and you create a "new" comfort zone.

"I Want My IBM Selectric Typewriter!

For example, I remember early in my career in the 1980's I worked in a clerical role for a large corporation. This was when computers were first being introduced to the workplace. I fought the change when I was first told that my job was going to be computerized and that the office would be going "paperless." First off, I didn't know what "paperless" meant and couldn't conceive in my mind how the office would function without the many files I was responsible for. I didn't like the idea. I couldn't imagine how I could do my job without all the papers and files that I worked with. I liked my IBM Selectric Typewriter and didn't want to give it up.

Then the computers arrived and I had to learn how to use them. At first it was very tedious and difficult and I didn't know what I was doing. However, once I began to learn it, I became very good at it and I saw how much easier it was going to make my job. Now I couldn't imagine life without my computer.

We have to identify our own personal coping mechanisms and develop the skills necessary to manage the changes that will come.

This is the reason the managing change and continuous skill building columns on the Resiliency Hourglass are critical to supporting the skills contained within the vessel. It is the critical foundation for the remainder of the material.

Once we experience the paradigm shift needed to understand the priority these supporting columns of the model brings, and they become ingrained into our behavior, we can then direct our attention to the top and bottom portions of the hourglass.

CHAPTER 8

Personal and Interpersonal Characteristics

When describing the vessel section of the hourglass, the top portion containing the personal characteristics is addressed first, followed by the bottom portion containing the interpersonal characteristics.

What I Need to Do for "Me"

Personal Characteristics: The top portion of the hourglass vessel represents the characteristics we need to develop resiliency at a personal level. These are the skills we need to manage ourselves as an individual; responsibility, goals and priorities and are represented by the "sand" that flows through the vessel from the top portion.

These personal characteristics, which begin the process of the "sand" flowing through the neck of the vessel from the top of the hourglass and in the order in which it flows, starts with responsibility, then goals and lastly, priorities.

What I Need to Do for "You"

Interpersonal Characteristics: The bottom portion of the hourglass represents the skills we need to learn at an interpersonal level to develop a resiliency. As the "sand" that represents the first three self-empowerment characteristics and the associated behaviors and skills beginning with "responsibility" first, then "goals," and lastly, "priorities" flows through the neck of the vessel to the base, it begins to "pile up" at the bottom of the base.

Once the first grain of sand representing "responsibility" "hits" the base it is then "transformed" into the first interpersonal trait of self-empowerment, which is "collaborate." It then continues with the next trait from the top, "goals;" which transforms to "empathy" upon hitting the base. Lastly, the "sand" representing "priorities" flows throw and transforms into the self-empowerment trait of "teamwork" which completes the process.

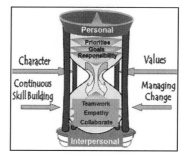

CHAPTER 9

Characteristic 5—Responsibility

The first skill represented by the "sand" flowing through the neck of the hourglass vessel and is the foundational characteristic of self-empowerment is **responsibility**. We need to accept responsibility for ourselves and our circumstances. We are proactive and not reactive.

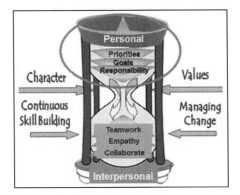

It's important to know the difference between the two. Dr. Stephen Covey describes this best in the *Seven Habits of Highly Effective People*.

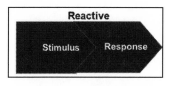

Reactivity

When we "react," it's like a knee-jerk reaction; we have no control over it and we go directly from that stimulus to response. It's a physical reaction. I get the stimulus and go right to the response. It's as if the two are "joined" together.

When we get distracted by things happening around us we are basically conditioned to respond in a particular way to a particular stimulus.

For example, a person who is reactive is negative towards change can demonstrate behaviors ranging from grudging compliance—moaning and groaning—to dysfunctional practices such as starting rumors and perhaps even sabotage.

Proactivity

"Concentrate on things where we have authority or control."

When we are proactive, we do not react to what's happening around us and accept responsibility for ourselves and our circumstances. We separate the "stimulus" from the "response." We do not put ourselves into the role of victim and we don't place blame on anything else. We concentrate on the things we can do something about; where we have authority or control.

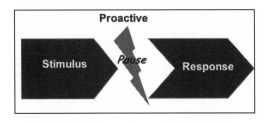

Separating the Stimulus from the Response

A person who is "proactive" *learns* how to separate the "stimulus" from the "response" and replace that with a "space" in the middle between the "stimulus" and the "response." Once they can do that they are in a better position for self-empowerment because they can look at the situation and make the best decision based upon the areas in which they have "'influence" or control.

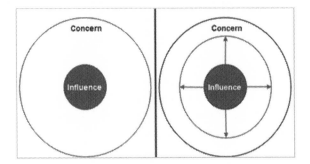

What "Circle" Am I In?

Circle of Concern/Influence: Dr. Covey illustrates this well through his model of the Circle of Concern and the Circle of Influence which is two circles; a smaller circle within a larger circle. The larger circle represents everything that a person could have a concern about. If a person concentrates his or her energies on issues within the larger Circle of Concern, he or she is dis-empowering themselves because there is nothing that they can do about those issues; they have no control or "influence" over them.

Who's in Control Here Anyway?

For example, I cannot control other people's behaviors; however, I can control my own. I cannot get to the other side of a brick wall by "banging" my head against it . . . I only get a headache. If I am not in a position of developing policies and procedures within an organization and I want to be an employee of that organization, I have to learn to "accept" those policies and procedures and learn how to adapt my behaviors and work performance to conform to them or accept the consequences of non-compliance; which might include being "fired" from my job. On the other hand, though I may not be able to change the policies and procedures; I am free to look for another job elsewhere. If I am not in a position of passing laws within the community, if I don't comply with those laws then I pay the consequences.

What is within my Circle of Influence? The end result of people focusing on the Circle of Concern is that they typically adapt an attitude of apathy because they feel powerless . . . or dis-empowered; however, they are dis-empowering themselves because they are choosing to focus their energies on the Circle of Concern and the things over which they have no power or control. They are unhappy and typically project a negative attitude towards everything they come in contact with, and, quite frankly, become a self-fulfilling prophesy.

The key is for a person to focus his or her energies on the smaller circle in the middle which represents everything which the person has "influence" or control over. The point is to concentrate on the things which a person has "influence" over; thereby avoiding the "stress" of focusing time and energy on things over which one has no control. When this is done, an interesting dynamic occurs on the smaller Circle of Influence—it causes the circle to grow larger; which cuts down on the size of the larger Circle of Concern.

The more we concentrate on the things that we have control over, the more power and influence we gain over our lives and this is a critical component to self-empowerment.

Endowments of the Human Personality

Returning to the proactivity model, acting within this "space" created by the separation of the "stimulus" and the "response," gives a person the "Freedom to Choose," based on the endowments of the human personality which all people possess: Self-awareness, Imagination, Conscience and Independent Will.

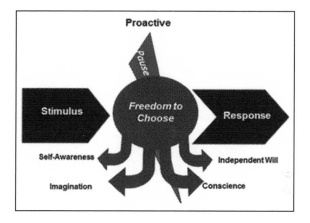

Self-Awareness: These are the things that a person knows about themselves; his or her likes, dislikes, habits, preferences, etc. For example, I know that I like chocolate ice cream. I know that I don't like lima beans. I know that I am easily distracted and need to work to focus. Everyone has those kinds of things that they know about themselves.

Imagination: People have the ability to be creative and develop alternatives in their mind. Once we have evaluated a situation, we have the ability to visualize various scenarios in our mind to evaluate the situation.

Conscience: The ability to distinguish between right and wrong, good and bad, etc., and is based on one's personal character and values.

Independent Will: All people have the ability to make choices based on their free will. They have the ability to evaluate the various alternatives in any given situation and make a decision based on their choice of the best way to respond.

Freedom of Choice—The "Space" in the Middle

When a person is proactive, he or she learns to develop the ability to separate themselves from their immediate reactions to a situation and make decisions based upon this freedom of choice, which is what will impact the result. This is where true empowerment begins.

For example, when a person loses his or her job as a result of downsizing and through no fault of his or her own, the first reaction is usually negative. They experience anger, depression and go through a process of blaming others, i.e., the company, their boss, their co-workers, etc. The reality of this, however, is that it doesn't do anything to rectify the situation and it's not a healthy way to react. That's not to say we deny the emotions we are experiencing, but rather find a positive way to deal with and address them; sometimes it can be just by taking the action of writing a resume and setting new career goals.

Proactivity, along with these four endowments, operates simultaneously and functions at a personal level as well as all in areas of our lives.

Applying all of this in our lives can be tricky. For example: personal health and wellness has always been a priority for me (self-awareness). While I do not consider myself a "health 'nut,'" I enjoy the benefits of being healthy and fit so I am extremely aware of nutrition and physical fitness and incorporating it into my lifestyle. As a result of this basic "mindset," I typically get all the recommended annual examinations and "screenings" considered necessary for basic health awareness, including the annual mammograms recommended for women. I had always been "used" to everything being "fine" and "normal" until about ten years ago when, as a result of one of these "routine" mammograms, a problem was identified.

Everything's Fine . . . I don't Think So

This was the first time I was diagnosed with breast cancer. With this first diagnosis, I underwent a lumpectomy and was told that "everything was 'fine;' they 'got it all.'" The recommended treatment was that I would just need radiation treatments and need to take medication for five years; I would not need chemotherapy or any other type of more aggressive treatment.

Throughout this entire time, it was a struggle to keep my concentration on the things I could "influence" (circle of influence) and not the many things that were of "concern" (circle of concern). I needed to focus on where I had control and power (freedom to choose). I had to learn "mental discipline" and focus my thoughts on telling myself, "What do I need to do right now . . . this minute?" Then I needed to be sure I was doing those things.

For example: Even though I was told the same thing by three of my doctors, I was not comfortable with what I was hearing (imagination/conscience); and sought out other medical opinions. As a result of the fifth medical consultation (independent will) it was discovered that what I had been told at first was incorrect; they had not "gotten it 'all,'" and I needed to have additional surgery. I had a second lumpectomy and after that I was truly cancer-free. However, my new doctor strongly recommended chemotherapy, and I agreed (independent will). I went through chemotherapy for five months, and then radiation treatments for approximately six weeks.

After Being "Cured" You're Not Supposed to Get "Sick" Again

Following my doctors' recommendations, I continued to faithfully undergo the annual mammograms. I was "cured" and everything was fine for about ten years (self-awareness/ independent will). Then, something like an "instant replay" occurred. After the annual mammogram I received the notice that I needed to have another biopsy; and that biopsy revealed another type of breast cancer; not a "relapse" of what I had ten years earlier, but a completely different type of breast cancer. This time I underwent a mastectomy, followed by three months of chemotherapy, a second mastectomy and reconstruction surgery.

Thirty-Seconds of Sympathy

I responded to the second occurrence in the same manner as I did the first. When informed that I would need to have chemotherapy again, I allowed myself 30 seconds to "feel sorry for myself" and shed one tear. I then moved on and focused on what I needed to do at that moment (independent will). I continued to focus on the things where I had "influence" and find something "positive" in it no matter what.

"Moonstruck Therapy

I call this *Moonstruck Therapy,* which is based upon the unforgettable "slap" scene in the movie *Moonstruck* with Cher and Nicholas Cage. In that scene, Cage's character had just told Cher's character that he loves her and she responds by "slapping" him across the face saying, "Snap out of it!" It's that simple. Sometimes being proactive means doing whatever we need to do to *"snap out of"* whatever is stopping us from moving forward and staying in the moment. This is not to deny that healing is needed when terrible things can and do happen to us. The point is to not "wallow" in the negativity and get "stuck" for extended periods of time. The key is to *"do"* whatever needs to be done to move forward. While everyone is different and may need differing lengths of time to work through their own unique issues, the key is to recognize where our influence is found and avail oneself of the various resources to resolve them.

In my own case, through all this, I learned that I can exercise proactivity and create new possibilities and positive alternatives for new opportunities. I can look at the situation objectively, identify the areas where I have some power and control, then focus my energy and actions on those areas. I can share my experiences of self-transformation and transition with others and help empower them to overcome the challenges and obstacles that they are facing in their lives. By teaching them how to empower themselves, the result is self-empowerment for me.

"New Habits" = *Self-Empowerment*

These principles apply to all areas of life: personal, work, family, community, etc., it's the application, or putting it into practice where the challenge lies. Are you struggling with self-management issues; time management, focusing, personal organization? Is there a difficult career or work situation you are dealing with? Are there family issues that are causing problems for you? The key is to separate the "stimulus" from the "response" and get in the habit of focusing on the things where you have some "influence" or control. There will always be times where we "react;" it is part of being human. The solution is to "recognize" when it's happening and then get back to focusing on where your "influence" is . . . and then "do" that. The more we continue to "do" that, as a result of the repetition, the new, possibly "uncomfortable" behaviors will soon become a part of our "comfort zone" and will then become new, "good habits" as opposed to the old "bad habits." As a step towards self-empowerment, try "practicing" one "new" habit every thirty days. After thirty days, those "new habits" are no longer new and we're well on our way towards self-empowerment.

To begin, the remaining characteristics, starting with "goals," are tools to keep us focused on those things where we have power and control and continuing to propel ourselves forward on the path towards self-empowerment.

CHAPTER 10

Characteristic 6—Goals

The second characteristic of self-empowerment represented by the sand flowing down the neck of the hourglass vessel is goals. In the best-selling book *Simplicity,* Bill Jensen says, ". . . top performers and 'most admired' companies had very clear goals and objectives. And they worked very hard to keep them clear . . . day in, day out." In order for them to do that "day in, day out" they know what's important to attain them.

My First Career Goal

In my case, I remember the day very well when I set my first career goal. It was early in my career when I was in the administrative role in a division of the Human Resource

Department at a very large corporation and I attended my very first professional development class. This was the first time I ever experienced this type of learning and from the moment the class started something "clicked" inside of me. In a split second, I set a goal. I said to myself, "That's what I want to do," as I watched the instructor who was teaching the class.

When the time came for me to have my "career development" conversation with my supervisor, I mentioned that I would like to eventually transfer into the Training Department. It took some time; however, after four years another administrative position became available in the Human Resource Training Department as a registrar and I accepted a lateral move into that role. My job was to register employees into the management training courses that were offered by the company. One of the first things I did in that role was to register myself in all the classes for which I was responsible.

I spent a total of three years in this role in varying capacities and learned everything I could about the department; logistics, facilities, materials, adult learning theory, course evaluation, design, development, evaluation, etc. It wasn't always easy and often I felt very discouraged. At the time there was a great deal of turmoil in the industry in which I worked and the organization had gone through several major reorganizations.

Who's the Boss Today?

Within these three years I had five different supervisors as a result of these reorganizations. Not all of these supervisors were "supportive" of me, my career development, or my goals. One of them actually told me that I would "'never' have that job!" That I "wasn't qualified" and that they'd "bet a month's pay" that it would never happen. However, that particular manager didn't last very long either. I have to say that particular manager was the "exception" and not the "norm." The majority of the supervisors I had were excellent and really believed in developing and supporting the members of their staff.

After three years in these various administrative roles, I was promoted into a first level management position in the area of training facilities management . . . not necessarily where I wanted to be, but still close to the classroom. The manager who promoted me into the role was a great manager, and, unfortunately, became ill and passed away not long after my promotion. In his absence it became necessary for me to report directly to the district manager.

The Performance Appraisal

When the time came for my first performance appraisal, I found myself in a rather "unique" position. This manager asked me to "write" my own appraisal and development plan. It's not very often a person gets an opportunity such as this and I gave myself "glowing" reviews along with a development plan that consisted of a career path for me to be promoted to corporate trainer. I "held my breath" when I handed in this appraisal . . . not knowing what his reaction would be.

When the time came for us to discuss my performance he told me that he was in agreement with everything I had written and thought that I would be an excellent trainer. He told me he supported my efforts. In the meantime he recommended me for another position where my responsibilities were designing, developing and evaluating training programs and excellent development towards a corporate trainer position. I was in this role for two years and then when the organization was increasing the staff of corporate trainers, he recommended me for the position, and I "got" it.

It took approximately ten years for my actual goal to materialize. However, I never lost sight of it and continuously took advantage of every self-development opportunity that was offered to me; even if it was not directly related to the goal. I never gave up and always maintained a "positive" and "focused" outlook; even when it appeared as if things were not going as I would have liked.

> *"Identify what is important to*
> *you—determine your life purpose."*

I later learned specific goal setting processes that I have put into practice, and from which self-empowerment emerges. It begins by developing our own, personal statement of purpose. Identifying what is most important in your life or your life's priorities is one of the first steps in beginning to create a statement of purpose. While I didn't have this when I set my original goal to be a corporate trainer and kept my goal in my mind; it's important that this statement of purpose be in writing and reviewed periodically to see if you are on track or straying off course. If you are, you need to identify what you need to do to get back on track.

In order to begin to establish that statement of purpose for self-empowerment, a person needs to know what his or her goals are; what is his or her sense of purpose? What are they supposed to be doing?

We need to know our purpose. Ask yourself; "what is my purpose?" It is important to know that. One way is to take some time alone and define what that "purpose" is. What is at the center of your life? It helps to begin to look at all the different parts of your life.

What "Hat" am I Wearing?

Life Parts: No one exists in a vacuum. Our lives are made up of different parts; these are the different hats we wear, or our "life parts." Like an actor in a movie when playing a part, it's important to define our life parts in order to successfully integrate them into our lives to achieve our purpose. An actor would never show up on a movie set for the first day of filming without having read the script. We need to understand what our part is when we look at the various parts of our life. We identify six or seven life parts that are based on the different roles in your life or the various "hats" you wear. It helps to list between 6-7 clearly defined life parts as shown in the example below:

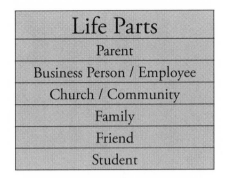

None of these Life Parts are totally separate from one another. They are all interconnected. If something affects one part of your life, it has an effect on all the others. We also influence others in all of these parts of our life.

Who Am I? What Am I About?

Purpose Statement: Having a statement of purpose helps us to stay focused on what is truly important. As the Cheshire Cat said to Alice in Wonderland when she asked him which way she should go "That depends a good deal on where you want to get to." To which Alice replied, "I don't much care where." "Then it doesn't matter which way you walk," said the Cat.

If we don't identify our own passion and develop our goals around that passion, we end up helping other people to achieve their goals; either working for a company in a mundane, dead-end job or in a profession we selected because we didn't know what we wanted to "do." Ultimately the end result is the same. We are left feeling unfulfilled ourselves.

We have to know where we want to go. As illustrated earlier in the Heart Model, everyone needs to identify where his or her "passion" or "drive within" is coming from.

According to Bruce Wilkinson who wrote the book, *The Dream Giver,* everyone has a dream for his or her life. He calls it a universal and powerful longing; a big dream. This activity will help to tap into what that big dream is for you.

Picture This . . .

It's important to have a clear sense of purpose of where you want your life to go. The first thing you want to do is get a clear picture in your mind of where you want your life to be. Take some time where it is "quiet" and you are alone. Get "comfortable" and "picture" yourself in a place where you feel peaceful and relaxed. Give yourself about five to ten minutes to think about your life. Picture yourself doing everything you always wanted to be doing. What are you thinking, doing, and feeling? What are some of the things you are saying and what are people saying to you? Think about your job, your family; what types of activities are you engaging in. What does this feel like?

After about five to ten minutes; stop. Now it's time to take about five minutes and continue with the remainder of the activity.

To do this you are to write as fast as you can. If you get blocked, keep writing. Write from the perspective of what the most important things in your life are. Project your life forward.

The rules for doing this are:

- This is a confidential activity
- Push through it. Do not stop to think about it, just keep writing. It might feel awkward, but that is okay; it is for your eyes only.

Relax, take a deep breath and get ready with pens, paper, or your computer. Set a timer for five minutes. Start the timer and respond to the following question: "What is your purpose?" And then "write" non-stop—do not edit or correct errors—just keep writing. If you get "blocked," push through it . . . until the timer goes off . . . and then STOP. You may be amazed at how fast those five minutes will go by. At the end of the five minutes, you will have the "beginning" of your purpose statement. At a future time you will want to fine-tune it; but this is the start—your "rough" draft.

Sample Purpose Statement

I am an advocate for people. I equip them with the tools they need to be successful in their businesses and careers.

I am a responsible mother and give priority to that role. I build productive relationships with family, friends, church, business, community and academic relationships.

In my professional life I produce results. I act with courage, consideration and discretion; build business partnerships and negotiate win/win agreements. I act with courage, consideration and discretion. I focus my life parts and goals; balancing home and career effectively.

Personal and professional learning, growth and development are a priority for me. I strive for excellence in education and continuously seek to further my educational and learning opportunities.

My home is a place where I find comfort, peace and happiness. I seek to create a clean, orderly environment, yet livable and comfortable.

I value good health and fitness and maintain an addiction-free lifestyle.

I'm committed to a clean, peaceful world, where all people live lives of joy and have fun.

SMART Criteria: Once our purpose has been identified, the next skill that needs to be developed for self-empowerment is setting goals to fulfill and support that purpose.

SMART Criteria

This is where we start to hone in and focus on what is truly important. We set long and short range goals for each life part. In business, for goals to be effective they need to meet SMART criteria. That means that they have to be:

- Specific
- Measurable
- Attainable
- Relevant
- Time-bound/Trackable

Supportive Goals

Goals are set to support your purpose. Goal setting is begun by setting and developing long and short-term goals for each part of your life. What do you want to accomplish in each of the various parts of your life? These goals are connected to our purpose. It is important to connect to our purpose. By connecting it means that we just take a minute or so and read over our purpose statement and reflect upon the end result. It does not take very long to do; however, it is important to do this at least once a week. An effective practice is to record it and download onto a CD or MP3 player and listen to it over and over again.

For each of your life parts, you want to begin by writing one short term and one long-term goal using the SMART criteria. Short term is something you want to accomplish within the next week or month. Long term is just that; it can be a year, or two, or five, etc.

A Goal isn't a Goal Unless it's Written Down

It is important to get used to the process of writing goals. By doing this it will aid you to begin seeing things differently; from the perspective of your goals and develop a clearer focus in attaining them through planning, organizing and managing your time.

Your goals for each of your Life Parts need to consist of the five basic categories: Resources, Action Steps, and Deadlines or "By-When" Dates, Success Indicators and Accomplishment Date.

Resources: These are the things you will use in accomplishing the goal. Who will help you? What tools you will use? Where you will obtain the financial backing or money you will use?

Action Steps: What are you going to do towards accomplishing this goal? How are you going to do it?

Deadlines or "By-When" Dates: These target dates are critical for success. They must be realistic; however, without them the chances are that the goal will never be achieved. If a deadline is "missed" then you set another realistic one;

but always set deadline or "by-when" dates so you can monitor your success as you proceed through the process.

Success Indicators: How do you know you're making progress towards the attainment of your goals? These success indicators act as benchmarks along the way so you know you're on track or, if you're off track, to get right back on.

Accomplishment Date: This is your "pat on the back" for a job well done. Be sure to "reward" yourself when you meet your goal and it is "complete!"

> *"Self-empowerment comes from knowing*
> *what our priorities are and where we are*
> *spending our time."*

This goal setting process is an invaluable step towards self-empowerment and it can be said is, "easier said than done." The interruptions and crises' of daily life happen to everyone. Just how does a person get everything done with everything happening at once? Self-empowerment comes from knowing what our priorities are and where we are spending our time.

CHAPTER 11

Characteristic 7—Priorities

This is where we begin to start looking at how we manage our time. The third part of the sand to funnel through the hourglass vessel is **priorities.** Self-empowerment comes from what we do with the time that we have. Are we using our time effectively or are we wasting the valuable time that we have?

Time is Money

The old adage that "time is money" is well understood. If we waste an hour a week for 52 weeks, we have wasted 52 hours in a year's time. Multiply that times the hourly rate and that is the amount of money the wasted time "costs" in a year. We don't have to dwell on it to understand the concept, and in all reality, I think it's safe to say most of us must "waste" more than one hour in a week's time.

Additionally, however, this doesn't take into account the amount of money we may have "lost" in the areas of possible missed opportunities. For example, contacting new customers, making higher commissions, increased revenues, possible promotions, etc.; there are endless possibilities of accomplishments that we may have achieved if we were effectively using our time. There's no way of knowing what opportunities may have been "missed."

"Should've, Would've, Could've" All Met in a Place Called "Didn't"

However, to avoid the *"should've's, would've's, could've's,"* which is a "negative" response and outside of out Circle of Influence, what we need to focus on is whether or not we are spending our time moving towards or away from accomplishing our goals. The key is to focus on activities that provide "leverage" towards attainment of our goals as opposed to "reacting" to external stimuli that we are being "bombarded with on a daily basis.

Chronos vs Kairos

Chronos/Kairos: Many people live a life of "survival" which consists of just doing what needs to be done in order to survive in the world. This is where the difference between Chronos and Kairos comes in. To clarify: this is not "good" vs. "bad;" it is making comparisons of the appropriateness and effects of them both. The key is to achieve balance between the two.

Chronos refers to the clock; it is linear; sequential. The "ticking" of the clock dictates the rhythm of our lives. It keeps us on track; we need to know what time to be at our job, when our appointments are scheduled; the necessities of life. This is not bad, and it is important. We have to take care of ourselves, eat right, get enough rest, exercise and respond to basic bodily functions; which mean to live a healthy lifestyle. This would also include dressing and grooming; which is all important. The key is <u>whether or not these things are ruling us</u>.

Kairos is the direction of your life. It is the quality; the value you get out of time as opposed to how many minutes or hours you put into it. It can be compared more to the "voice of direction" we get from a GPS. Are you moving in the direction you want your life to be going? Are you listening to the "voice" of your internal GPS and accomplishing the things you want to accomplish? Kairos time is the value you get out of life—the quality time or appropriate time.

The GPS vs the Clock

"There is a gap between what is valuable to us and how we spend our time."

For many of us there is a gap between the GPS and the clock—between what is valuable to us and how we spend our time. We spend our life as if a "stopwatch" has started and we're "racing" to "beat the clock."

During the 1960's at the New York World's Fair the thought was that the biggest challenge in the 21st century would be what people would do with all the spare time they would have. What happened? That's a rhetorical question. However, it could be suggested no one thought about the changing mindsets in society of more . . . better . . . faster. With the technology available now in the 21st Century, one person can do the work that ten/twenty people did in the 20th Century. However, there's more work to do. People are working fifty and sixty-hour workweeks and are "stressed" to the max just to survive.

But I'm "Working" as Hard and as Fast as I Can!

Efficiency vs. Effectiveness: This is where we begin to look at being efficient versus being effective.

Efficiency means to do things right. It is the stopwatch; how we spend our time—the countdown. However, the problem with efficiency is that it focuses on "doing." We are always doing something. However, if you are always "doing," what kind of fruits will you produce (reap)?" A: busyness, stress, too much to do and not enough time to do it.

Effectiveness means to do the right things. It is the GPS; am I going in the direction I want to be going to "reap" the harvest I want to "reap?" It keeps me focused on "doing" the things that are important towards achieving my goals.

Approaching life from a Kairos viewpoint encompasses and includes the necessities, the reality of life, (Chronos) while keeping what is important (Kairos) in front.

Living life in Kairos time entails identifying the activities that provide us with the "leverage" we need in order to attain our goals in our lives and careers. Focus on performing high-payoff activities—those that will provide the best return on your time investment. Always ask yourself, "Is this the best use of my time right now?"

Leverage vs Reactivity

Leverage/Reactivity: In the earlier section on **responsibility,** we covered the importance of remaining focused and concentrating on acting upon the things that we have some power and control over was covered. The point is to concentrate on the things that are within our Circle of Influence and not react to the pressures being imposed by the surrounding environment.

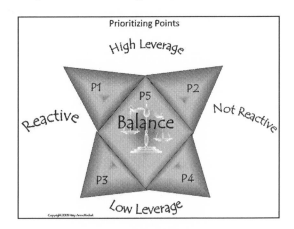

The **Prioritizing Points** model is based on two elements: **leverage**; defined by Merriam Webster as:

- *Leverage: "1 LEVERAGE Function: noun; 1: the action of a lever or the mechanical advantage gained by it 2: power, effectiveness <trying to gain more political leverage>3: the use of credit to enhance one's speculative capacity*
- *2 LEVERAGE Function: transitive verb Inflected Form(s): -aged; -ag•ing To provide (as a corporation) or supplement (as money) with leverage; also: to enhance as if by supplying with financial leverage."*

For our purposes, the focus is on the first bullet, number two, power effectiveness. This is what gives us our power and effectiveness in achieving self-empowerment in managing our time, or for that matter, "our life." That power is based on our purpose statement and our goals, the things that are "important" to us. Activities that have leverage are activities that are aligned to our purpose statement and are moving us in the direction of achieving our goals. What it comes down to is what is important.

The second element in the model is "reactive." The definition follows:

> *Reactive: "1: of, relating to, or marked by reaction or reactance. 2: a: readily responsive to a stimulus; b: occurring as a result of stress or emotional upset "reactive depression"*

The focus here is on number two; a: *responding to a stimulus that is imposed by the environment and b: occurring as a result of stress or emotional upset.* These are the activities that are urgent; that we have to respond to. Urgent means, *"Calling for immediate action: pressing."* These are the events and things that happen in life that we have to respond to.

Priorities

These elements combine to create four prioritizing points:

Point 1 (P1) represents the combination of "high leverage" and "reactive." This means any activities relating to this point are "high leverage" because they are related to our purpose and goals and are "reactive" because they are being imposed by the environment and we have to respond, and sometimes react quickly. These are crises, sudden problems, deadlines, etc.

Point 2 (P2) represents the combination of "high leverage" and "not reactive." These activities are the activities needed for self-empowerment because they are "high leverage," meaning they are related to our purpose and goals and are "not reactive" because they do not have to be addressed immediately; there is no outside pressure from the environment to do them.

Point 3 (P3) represents the combination of "reactive" and "low leverage." These activities are "reactive" because there is a sense of urgency being imposed by the environment. It's a sudden crisis that must be dealt with. However, they are "low leverage" because they are not related to our purpose and goals. They are the interruptions that get us off track. These are "other people's issues (OPI's)." The old saying, "Lack of planning on your part does not constitute an emergency on my part," relates to these P3 issues.

Point 4 (P4) represents the combination of "low leverage" and "not reactive." This means that the activities are not related to our purpose and goals and are "not reactive" because they do not have to be addressed immediately; there is no outside pressure to do them. These are our time wasters; our escape activities.

I'll "Do It" Tomorrow

Self-empowerment comes from learning to spend the majority of our time in P2 because we're working on things that are related to our purpose and are related to our goals.

What usually happens, for instance, is that this is where we procrastinate. We put the activities in P2 off; then they "jump" into P1 and we become reactive and have to respond to the urgency.

When most of the things we have to accomplish are in a crisis mode, we have more and more things that we have to respond to that are crisis driven. Then, when we finally get a break we're so beaten up by the stress of being in crisis mode, we *escape* into P4 and engage in "coping-types" of behaviors and activities.

The key is to focus on activities that fall into the P2 area. We will always have crisis situations that we will have to respond to; however, when we handle the situations while they are in P2, we will have less jumping over into P1.

When P3 activities come up, we handle them and get back to "high leverage" activities. Whenever possible we avoid engaging in activities that fall into P3 and P4.

Being human, we will always have experiences where we drop into P4. Following is an example of how this has happened to me.

"Crash" Goes the Plant

Early in my career when I was working in the training department of that very large corporation, I did a great deal of my course-preparation work at home.

One day when I was working from home at my kitchen table, I was feeling pretty good about the progress I was making. When it became time for lunch, I took a break and had lunch. After I finished my lunch, I was cleaning up the dishes and I noticed that the leaves on the plant that was hanging over the kitchen sink were "growing" towards the window and that the plant needed to be turned around so the plant would "grow" evenly. It was just a "minor" distraction and without thinking very much of it, I turned the plant around and hung it back up on the hook.

Then I sat back down at the kitchen table and resumed my work. Within about two minutes there was a loud crash! The plant that I had just hung up had fallen down into the sink and "spilled" out completely in the sink. It turns out, since I had "hastily" responded to the "minor" distraction, I had not put it back on the hook securely enough and it slipped and fell off the hook.

Now I had to stop what I was doing and clean up the mess, (that I had created based upon a "minor distraction), and put the plant securely back on the hook; which was a "waste" of time. Then I resumed my work.

This instance is an example of P1; it was a crisis that occurred and, even though it was of my own "making," I had to deal with it immediately. It was related to my purpose; my purpose statement says: "My home is a place where I find comfort, peace and happiness. I seek to create a clean, orderly environment, yet livable and comfortable." It was definitely related to a clean, orderly environment. However, when I think about it now, how important was it at that moment that I "fix" the plant? In all reality, it was a minor distraction that took me away from my work. If I had left it alone the crisis wouldn't have happened. There was no "pressing" reason that plant had to be "turned" around at that particular time . . . It could have waited until a time when I was performing household chores and **NOT** when I was "supposed" to be working . . . even though technically I was still on my lunch break. I had to stop my work and clean up a "mess," that, if I had "left it alone, wouldn't have occurred in the "first place." Lesson learned . . . *stay focused*.

"I Work Best Under Pressure!" vs. Are You An Arsonist?

Something to address here, however, is how often we may have to "clean up" a "mess" that we created. For example . . . when we procrastinate, which means . . .

when we "put off" doing something that we "know" we "should" be doing *__"NOW"__* until the last minute. Then, under the "pressure" of "being under the 'gun,'" we have to "rush" to meet the "deadline." I can't count how many times a student or client has said to me something like: "I don't have time to plan or organize; I'm too busy "putting out fires!" Or, "I work best "'under pressure!'" Then they look like a "hero" because they "put out the 'fire.'" However, if they had not waited until the last minute there would have been "no 'fire'" in the first place. I call people who engage in these types of behaviors "arsonists," because, while they are successful in solving the problem or "putting out the fires," should they be "rewarded" for solving problems that they created, or "putting out 'fires'" that they started?

Ask yourself the question: "Am I an arsonist?" Where in the course of your day are you creating problems that you know you will have to "solve" later?

The "Battle" of the TV vs My Exercise Video

However, that being said and getting back to my earlier example, after cleaning up the "mess" from the plant, I went on to complete my work. I finished at the time I had planned and then proceeded to get ready to do my exercise video. I changed into my workout clothes; turned on the television and began to access my exercise video. However, I became distracted again by a television program that was on at that time while the video was being accessed. And there I sat, completely mesmerized by this daytime television program. I dropped from P2 right into P4. At that point, however, I completely knew what I was doing! In that moment I experienced a "turning point." I realized that I faced a choice. I could choose to sit there, stay in P4 and watch this program, or I could lift myself back up to P2 and complete my exercise program. I am proud to say that I turned off the television and I completed my exercise program.

The point is . . . once we experience the paradigm shift and live our life from our Purpose and not the whims of the environment; we know what we are doing. Distractions and interruptions will come, "plants" will "fall," television programs will be on . . . however; when we develop an increased awareness of all our activities, after a while you will not let yourself get away with wasting your time. We all have the exact same number of minutes in a day. It's how we each choose to use them that makes the difference. Don't sabotage your purpose.

Walking the "Tightrope" of Life: Achieving Balance

Prioritizing Point Five (P5) Balance: The center of the model represents the fifth point: "balance." This is where we begin moving towards living in Kairos Time. The image of the uneven scale at the center of the model represents the fact that we will never be equally balanced in all of these points. In reality, we do not want to be. The key to self-empowerment is to find the right "balance" that works for you. This is balancing all the interruptions that occur in the course of a day and being flexible enough to determine the appropriate behaviors to exhibit when they occur.

Kairos time comes from the quality of living life in the "moment." It comes from the center of the "Heart" model and where your "passion" lies. It is derived by determining which activities and functions you engage in are high leverage and contribute towards the attainment of your goals; concentrating on them and avoiding those that do not. Once you learn how to schedule and balance your time between activities that are reactive and high leverage and focus on living your "passion" during the course of each day Kairos Time will emerge . . . . One way to tell is that sometimes there is no sense of "time," or the "clock;" it is as if time is "flying by," but it doesn't feel like it. You may feel "energized," or a new sense of accomplishment in completing your day-to-day activities.

We all have to deal with the interruptions and crises of daily life and self-empowerment comes from employing tools to help us manage our activities and our time. We have already started the process of accepting responsibility and clarifying our purpose and setting goals for the different life parts.

An important skill to develop is the habit of documentation; which means recording our activities and accomplishments as well as the planning and scheduling of our time.

Periodically we have to set some time aside to review our purpose statement and our long-term goals; once a year is usually good for this; or any time of "transition" or change. Spend some time reviewing your accomplishments and visualize yourself attaining your goals. However, how many times can it seem so clear when we're in "planning" mode; and then everything falls apart when we get back into our old routines and fall back into our old habits.

How can we minimize the effects of this? There are always going to be things that happen. A good habit related to self-empowerment is to recognize and accept that rescheduling will happen, no matter how much planning is done.

I Don't Have Time to Plan . . .

There's an old saying that goes: *"If you fail to plan, you plan to fail."* If you want to succeed in achieving your goals, learning how to plan and schedule your time is a necessary skill.

Planning and Scheduling: Scheduling and planning is an important part of managing time. There are many different planners and organizers available on the market; they can be paper-based or electronic, however, a planner only works as well as it is put to use. All anyone needs to do is find a process and a tool that works for them. Self-empowerment comes from using a process . . . it is the process that works, not the tool.

A good process is yearly, monthly, weekly and daily planning. Additionally, it helps to create some sort of follow up system so that things do not fall through the cracks.

The following pages provide some suggested "examples" for planning and scheduling. For some people, just a monthly calendar will work—others may find that the weekly process works. Through trial and error a person needs to find for themselves what will work and customize it for his or her own use.

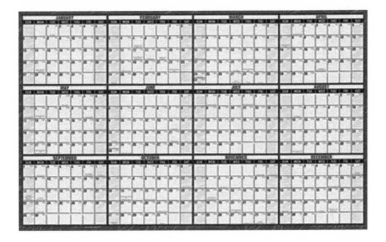

Yearly Planning: A yearly calendar works well to begin with. Once a year, usually around September or October is a good time to begin planning for the following year. A basic calendar works just fine, or a generic "datebook" on up to a more elaborate "planner" or electronic "calendar"—what works is up to each individual. Some people have a "work" and "personal" calendar. It is recommended to "coordinate" both the personal and professional schedules—it helps to know what appointments, meetings and events are scheduled, i.e., vacation, birthdays, holidays, etc. From a "holistic" perspective, it helps to integrate both personal and professional scheduling of events. This will avoid scheduling "conflicts" regarding work and family commitments.

Any kind of master/yearly calendar will do for this process. Some people find that a large "wall" calendar is good; others use a planner or electronic media. The type of calendar is not important; what is important is to have one.

Follow ups: This is a process for planning and scheduling of future events and activities. On the yearly calendar, an entry is made for any scheduled events on the appropriate month and date. During the course of the year, events and activities are added to the calendar as necessary. As a part of the monthly planning process, these activities get transferred to the appropriate Monthly Planning sheet to be transferred to the Weekly Lever when completing planning for that month.

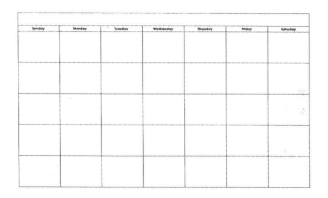

Monthly Planning: Towards the end of each month, review the plans and activities for the following month. Also, review what was accomplished the previous month. What was completed? What was planned and not accomplished or completed? Reschedule what was left unfinished or not accomplished, or reevaluate whether or not it is something that really needs to be done. How important is it? Is it critical to your Purpose?

Monthly planning sheets can be used to include Follow-ups or reminders for that month. They can also be used to record significant accomplishments or key information to retain.

Weekly Planning: The end of each week is the time for weekly planning for the following week. Ideally it is completed sometime between Friday afternoon and Sunday evening; preferably at a time when one has some" quiet time" to oneself. This is a good time to review one's "Purpose Statement" as a reminder to keep it "alive" and right "in front."

The Weekly Calendar aids in planning the week. It does not need to be an "actual" calendar; the idea is to aid in planning all activities and functions that need to be accomplished within that week. For some people it works to use their monthly calendar for scheduling; others whose scheduling needs might be more complex might want to use an actual weekly calendar with the timeframes listed.

Weekly Lever: The "Weekly Lever." is a tool designed to assist in remaining focused. It lists the separate life parts and the list of things to be accomplished for the week.

Short-term goals are listed in the "life parts" section on the left side—these are the overall goals for that week that apply to that particular life part.

On the right side, in the "Things to Do" section, all the things to be accomplished that week are written. A helpful suggestion is to use a colored highlighter as a way to cross them out. This results in providing a "visual" image of accomplishments as they are completed. A different color is used for whatever is left undone; which can then be reevaluated as to whether or not it is something that is truly a necessary activity—Is this something that "really" needs to be done or not? If yes, it gets carried to the next week, or rescheduled at another time—if no, it gets taken off the list.

The point of these planning sheets is to get into the habit of planning. Habits are formed by the continuous repetition of a specific behavior. At first it will "feel" uncomfortable, however, after a period of time, typically about 30 to 60 days; it becomes more and more comfortable until it becomes second-nature, or a "habit."

Not all people will use planning sheets such as these. The illustrations are included to provide a general idea of what the process entails. The idea is to develop a process that will work for each individual person; and some people can successfully keep track of all of these things "in their head," which is just fine. This provides the "framework;" and the person creates the "system" that will work for them.

Living in Karos Time
Today's Plans

Day:............. Date:...................

Prioritizing Points   *Today's   Schedule*

Living in Karos Time
Today's Notes

What "Day" is it Today?

Daily Plans: On a daily basis, the activities that need to be accomplished each day get transferred from the "Weekly Lever" to the "Daily Page" for the current day. A daily plan sheet is created for every day in the week to record two types of activities: time sensitive and time flexible.

Time Sensitive activities are the things that are scheduled for a specific time; specific appointments, client meetings, classes, etc. This is the "scheduling" part of the day and they are indicated on the right column in the appropriate block of time, i.e., client meeting is from 9:00-10:00 am. Travel time is also calculated, for example 6:45-7:15 to commute to work. That time is also blocked out. The blocks of time that are not filled in are used for time flexible activities.

Time Flexible activities are the things that have to get done, but not necessarily at a specific time; grocery shopping, correspondence, paying bills, etc. This is the "To Do" list.

What Do I Need to Do Now?

Activity Status: Time flexible activities are the "To Do" list. All the activities that need to be completed; i.e., write client proposal, return phone calls, answer emails, bill paying, order office supplies, etc. Upon completion of an activity, cross it off the list with one color highlighter; use a different color highlighter for what is not completed; which gets carried to the next day. Some suggestions might be as follows:

POSSIBLE HIGHLIGHTER STATUS "COLORS"	
YELLOW	COMPLETED
GREEN	"GO" TO TOMORROW
BLUE	PENDING
PINK	CANCELLED

Where Did I Put That "Yellow Sticky Note?"

Today's Notes: The reverse sides of the "Daily Plans" page are for any notes or reminders that need to be recorded for that day, i.e., phone messages, directions, or any information that is needed for "quick" reference. This is to eliminate all those little "sticky" notes that tend to get lost.

"Self-empowerment involves the discipline
to get back on track."

Learning processes such as these might feel awkward and difficult, if not "impossible" to fit into a personal "routine" initially. However, self-empowerment like anything new, after time, personal discipline and commitment, can become habitual, and therefore, as explained earlier, they become easier over time. In all reality, upon occasion, the process will not be completed, if not "forgotten." However, times like that are when it is time for a renewed "commitment." Self-empowerment involves the discipline to get back on track. On other occasions, an activity may be completed that is not "on the list." In cases such as this, you may choose to "record" it afterwards so the activity is "documented" if needed for future reference.

Rescheduling? Now What?

Putting it all Together—How it Works: Planning is a tool; not bondage. Some people may find that they do not need to have a daily schedule or written list of things to do. It might be more appropriate for another person to use a weekly system. The key is to find the process that works for the individual. We all need to recognize that we can do the best job planning and then "life happens" and "messes" up our plans. As the old saying goes, "that's why there are 'erasers' on the ends of pencils." If you use a paper-based tool you might want to use pencil when preparing your schedule; it's easier to "erase" and "reschedule" activities. It is important to have "flexibility" and the ability to "roll with the punches" when interruptions occur.

Discernment in the split-second of choice: Often time's things "happen" and we have to make a "split-second" decision with little time to think about it. In all reality, we may be saying "yes" to too many things and "no" to not enough things. There is a saying: "The enemy of the 'best' is the 'good.'" How do we discern what to say "yes" to and what to say "no" to?

This is where it may be necessary to reread your purpose statement. That is what determines what you say "yes" to. Say "no" to anything that is not related to your purpose.

"NO! I Can't Be In Two Places at the Same Time!"

Priorities can be tough; sometimes one can be conflicting with another. How do you make a determination? Refer back to your purpose statement. Which one of these priorities is going to provide the most leverage in moving you towards the accomplishment of your goals?

In his best-selling book, *'Getting Things Done: The Art of Stress-Free Productivity,* David Allen says: "Obviously many factors must be considered before you feel comfortable that you have made the best decision about what to do and when. "Setting priorities" in the traditional sense of focusing on your long-term goals and values, though obviously a necessary core focus, does not provide a practical framework for a vast majority of the decisions and tasks you must engage in day to day. Mastering the flow of your work at all levels you experience that work provides a much more holistic way to get things done and feel good about it."

We All Get the Same 24-Hour Day

While this is a "no-brainer," when I was first diagnosed with breast cancer, I had already completed my list of many high priority goals I wanted to accomplish that year. All those goals had to be put "on hold" for a year while I underwent the treatment for cancer . . . three major operations, chemotherapy, etc. I still had my goals, the priorities "shifted" as the greater priorities of fighting cancer arose and were dealt with. There was no question . . . I was able to keep my goals in sight. Sometimes "stuff happens" and you just need to "do what you've got to do" and "deal" with it appropriately and "in the moment." As the old saying goes, "life happens when you have other plans."

What "Part" Are You Willing to "Give Up."

Big Rocks: To summarize and tie all the pieces together, the following "story" illustrates nicely how it works. This "story" has been circulating on the Internet for many years; however, I first heard it over twenty years ago in a training class on Dr. Stephen Covey's Third Habit, "First Things First." It goes like this: A professor was giving a talk and he reached under the desk and brought out a large, clear bucket. Then he reached down and brought out a pile of big rocks and gently placed them in the bucket. He then asked the students; "Is the bucket full?" To which they responded, "Yes."

He shook his head and said, "No, you're wrong." Then he reached down and brought out a container of gravel and poured it into the bucket. The gravel filled in the large spaces between the big rocks. He asked the class again; "Is the bucket full?" To which they responded, "Yes."

He shook his head again and said, "No, you're wrong again." Then he reached down and brought out a container full of sand and poured it into the bucket. The sand filled the little spaces between the gravel and the big rocks. He then asked the class; "Is the bucket full?" Now they were beginning to get a little wise to his game; however, most of the students still said, "Yes."

He shook his head again and said, "No, you're wrong again." Then he reached down and brought out a bottle of water and poured the water into the bucket until it came to the top. Then he asked the class; "Is the bucket full?" "Yes," they all replied.

He smiled and said, "You're finally right! But what's the point?" The students looked at one another. They had no idea.

He said, "The point is, if I had put the water, the sand and the gravel in first; would I have been able to get the big rocks in? "No," they replied.

That's the point. *The key is to put the big rocks in first.* The big rocks represent the parts in our lives; the things that are important and the ones that provide leverage towards the achievement of our goals. When we put them first, the other, smaller things all find a place between them.

Summary: This completes the "Personal" section of the hourglass model; the characteristics and skills necessary for self-empowerment: "responsibility," "goals," and "priorities."

Self-empowerment comes from "mastering" these characteristics along with the related behaviors and skills. No one person can perfectly adhere to all of these at the same time; the point is that, when we get off track, we recognize it and get right on track again. As women it is even more critical to be organized and focused because we are "judged" more harshly than men based on the negative stereotypes projected by society. This is how we will continue to learn, grow and empower ourselves to remain focused and become "unstoppable" in achieving our goals. In truth, many women are well prepared when it comes to managing their time on the job because they have had to master this skill in order to handle the demands of home and family life.

CHAPTER 12

Interpersonal Characteristics

The focus of this chapter is on the bottom section of the hourglass model; the "Interpersonal" piece. This is a critical part for women because if mishandled, they run the risk of being stereotyped negatively at an even higher level.

If "They" Would Just Get Their "Act Together!

This is the part of self-empowerment where it can be much more difficult because it pertains to the relationships we have with other people, institutions and organizations. This can be *frightening* since we have less control in this arena because the only area in which we have 100% control is with ourselves. Often the tendency is to want the other person to change, so we don't have to—thereby remaining in our own comfort zone.

In addition, as women another challenge we might encounter here is that we are also experiencing some of the effects of being stereotyped by some of the people with whom we need to interact. The characteristics and related skills needed to manage our relationships with other people are: collaborate, empathy and teamwork.

The following chapters cover the skills and characteristics associated with developing relationships and communicating effectively as a leader, beginning with the first characteristic which is "collaborate" and the self-empowering skills and behaviors associated with it.

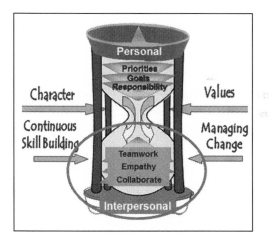

CHAPTER 13

Characteristic 8—Collaborate

The term "collaborate" represents a "shift" in the mindset that as an individual I may not have all the answers and I need to learn to seek out and communicate with other people to get the answers I need. To do this I need to shift my mindset to one of a win/win attitude in which, not only do I want to achieve my goals, I also want to help others achieve their goals. Assertiveness, negotiating, and conflict resolution skills are a must in this arena. I must be able to work with others and develop solutions that will benefit all of us.

Communications

As a self-empowered woman, I may need to examine my communication style and determine if I am communicating effectively. This is an area in which the negative stereotypes are exaggerated when it comes to women. I need to be aware if I am being too aggressive or I risk being perceived as one or more of the "tough," "masculine" or "angry" stereotypes. If I'm too passive when making requests or attempting to influence others, then I run the risk of having the "weak" or "emotional" stereotypes assigned to me. Assertive behaviors will aid in my authenticity in adapting my communication style to the individual circumstances.

Assertiveness

Assertiveness is a form of self-expression in which a person learns to stand up for his or her own rights without violating the rights of others. It meets three criteria:

1. It is appropriate to the person(s) and situation involved
2. It respects one's own basic human rights
3. It respects the human rights of others.

Appearing Confident and Competent

When a person is communicating assertively, they appear more confident and competent. They express their thoughts and feelings in a way that is appropriate and respectful of everyone involved. In addition, they also respectively and actively listen to others when appropriate. However, we must also be aware that there can be a "slippery slope" between being perceived as "confident" and "arrogant." Be careful not to "go over-the-top" and appear egotistical when you are actually feeling "insecure." Self-empowerment is developed by "being yourself."

To develop assertiveness skills we first must be aware of our own behavior. We need to learn how to be both diplomatic and assertive.

Assertiveness vs Aggressiveness

Assertiveness is not aggressiveness and it is a misconception that assertive people are aggressive. In fact, much of the assertiveness training I've done has been with people who were "perceived" as "aggressive" in their communications style who wanted to learn assertive communications techniques. Therefore, it's important to understand that when talking about becoming assertive, I'm not only talking about moving from passive to assertive, but also moving from aggressiveness to assertiveness.

Influencing Behaviors

It is important to first understand where our current behaviors came from, before we can effectively change them and adapt to our situation when necessary. Most of our behavioral styles originate from early "scripting" that has been imprinted on us by the authority figures in our life—parents, teachers and older siblings. We can re-write the script when it doesn't serve us any more. To learn assertiveness skills I may need to "shift" from my "comfort zone" and develop some of these new skills to aid in my interpersonal effectiveness. The illustration following presents a basic model of interpersonal behaviors that that are typically used to attempt to influence the behavior of others.

This model is based on two elements on a scale of "high" to "low: Concern for "self," or "my needs," and Concern for "others" needs. These elements combine to illustrate four separate behaviors:

- High concern for my needs and low concern for others (aggressive): These behaviors are where a person puts their needs above those of others. They can sometimes be referred to as the "steamroller" because of the forcefulness of their expressions. This person projects a "win/lose" attitude in their approach to communications. This is the person who has to be "right" all the time, etc. Negative stereotypes that might be assigned to women exhibiting these types of behaviors could be "tough," "masculine," "angry" or even the "ice queen."

• Low concern for other's needs and low concern for mine (passive aggressive): The person who exhibits the passive aggressive behaviors will appear to have concern for others, however will not exhibit those behaviors and sometimes even "sabotage" the other person's efforts to meet their own needs. There are many negative expressions for these behaviors which will not be expanded upon here because of the negativity involved. Negative stereotypes that might be assigned to women exhibiting these types of behaviors could be "weak," conniving," or possibly "emotional."

• High concern for others' needs and low concern for mine (passive): Passive behaviors are where the individual sacrifices his or her own needs and rights in an attempt to satisfy the needs and rights of the other person. This is the person that is sometimes referred to as the "doormat" because they allow themselves to be "walked" on. They put themselves in a lose/win position because they allow themselves to "lose" and the other person "wins." Negative stereotypes that might be assigned to women exhibiting these types of behaviors are the same as the passive aggressive style because they "appear" the same.

• High concern for my needs and high concern for others' (assertive): Assertive people balance a high concern for their needs with a high concern for the needs of the other person. They project a win/win attitude and communicate that everyone's needs are important and valued.

Bill of Assertive Rights

In his classic book on Assertiveness Training, *When I Say No, I Feel Guilty,* Dr. Manuel J. Smith, Ph.D. lists what he calls "A Bill of Assertive Rights:"

1.	I. You have the right to judge your own behavior, thoughts, and emotions, and to take the responsibility for their initiation and consequences upon yourself.
2.	You have the right to offer no reasons or excuses for justifying your behavior.
3.	You have the right to judge if you are responsible for finding solutions to other people's problems.
4.	You have the right to change your mind.
5.	You have the right to make mistakes—and be responsible for them.
6.	You have the right to say, "I don't know."
7.	You have the right to be independent of the goodwill of others before coping with them.
8.	You have the right to be illogical in making decisions.
9.	You have the right to say, "I don't understand."
10.	You have the right to say, "I don't care."
11.	You have the right to say no, without feeling guilty.

By applying these "rules" and learning assertive behaviors, we can learn to "cope" effectively with the many conflicts we experience in everyday living and reside in the top right corner of the model of assertiveness with high concern for ourselves and high concern for others.

Conflicts!

Conflicts can occur in interpersonal communications and these behaviors apply to how we manage the resolution of conflicts we encounter every day. Conflict occurs when parties with contrasting goals come in contact with one another and the conflict resolution styles track with the assertive behaviors. When "misused," They can result in the same negative stereotypes being projected onto a woman who is engaging in them.

The key to successful conflict resolution is to engage in assertive behaviors and remain open to the opinions of others.

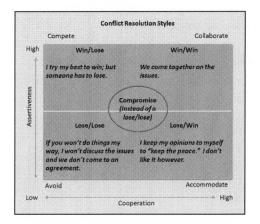

The Thomas-Kilmann Conflict Mode Instrument developed by Kenneth W. Thomas and Ralph H. Kilmann, describes five different Conflict Resolution Styles. These "styles" are based upon the description of a combination of two distinct behaviors: "Cooperation" and" Assertiveness." These two behaviors are illustrated on an axis from "high" at one end of the axis, to "low" at the other end of the axis as shown in the above diagram. These behaviors "combine" to describe the behaviors listed in the table below:

Behavior	Description
High Cooperation/ Low Assertiveness	Accommodating Behaviors (Lose/Win)
Low Cooperation/ Low Assertiveness	Avoidance Behaviors (Lose/Lose)
High Assertiveness/ Low Cooperation	Competing Behaviors (Win/Lose)
High Assertiveness/ High Cooperation	Collaborative Behaviors (Win/Win)
Middle Assertiveness/ Middle Cooperation	Compromising Behaviors

Lose/Win: Accommodating behavior, high cooperation, low assertiveness. A person who demonstrates this conflict resolution style is someone who puts another person's needs before their own in an attempt to avoid conflict. This is the person who cancels his or her vacation because a co-worker needs to take the time off at the last minute or takes on additional assignments unrelated to his or her role while their colleagues engage in other activities.

As with the "passive" assertive behavior, people engaging in the behaviors associated with this conflict resolution style are sometimes referred to as "doormats" because other people "walk all over" them. This is a common style for many women who have been acculturated by society to be "caregivers" and "nurturers." Often these people feel resentful and angry because their needs and concerns are typically not addressed; however they withhold their true feelings and do not express what they truly want.

Lose/Lose: Avoidance behavior, which is low cooperation, low assertiveness. The person who engages in this conflict resolution style is someone who will not communicate at all. They withdraw into themselves something like a "turtle" going into its shell. There is no concern for their needs or the needs of the other person. In this case both parties "lose" because there is no communication and no possible options are explored.

Win/Lose: Competing behavior, high assertiveness, low cooperation is a conflict resolution style where one person "has" to lose. While completely appropriate in many instances, such as competitive sports, etc., in interpersonal communications it is not always the best solution. As with the aggressive behavior described in the assertiveness styles, the person who demonstrates the competing behaviors can sometimes be perceived as a "steamroller," because they "roll" over others based on their own needs, opinions, etc. They can sometimes be perceived as "demanding," "self-centered," or even "cold" and "uncaring," which can also result in the "ice queen" stereotype being projected onto women engaging in these types of behaviors.

Compromise: With this behavior, each person attempts to gain concessions from the other by giving up a little bit, in order to get the other party to give up a little bit and "meeting in the middle," or "finding middle ground," to avoid a Lose/Lose and find a workable solution.

Dr. Manuel "Pete" Smith refers to this as a "workable compromise." He says that a compromise does not have to be "fair;" it just has to work.

Win/Win: Collaborative Behavior, high assertiveness, high cooperation is a conflict resolution style where the person demonstrates true concern for both the needs of the other person as well as his or her own. The attitude is that an agreement can be reached that will satisfy both parties if they can share ideas and develop a mutual solution.

The behaviors demonstrated in the conflict resolution styles are situational; meaning that in certain situations one may be more appropriate for various circumstances. However, each person has his or her own preferred conflict resolution style; which works just fine in the appropriate circumstances, yet, may not serve them well when the situation would be better managed with another style.

Self-empowerment comes from developing the ability to assess the situation and adapt our behavior to respond appropriately to the situation at hand. The first step in attaining this is to recognize one's own preferred conflict resolution style. Then, when confronted with a conflict situation, assess the situation and determine which behavior is the best to employ in that instance. In most cases, our main challenge will be when employing behaviors that are outside of our "comfort zone," or one of our "less preferred" styles.

It is important to recognize that everyone's conflict management style is not the same. While you may not "know" what another person's "style" is, by observing their behaviors you can often get an idea of how to best approach the situation. Additionally, with individuals with whom you interact often or have a standing relationship you might want to consider discussing how they prefer to approach these types of situations. This might provide you with an idea of what their preferred conflict management "style" is. It might also "open" up channels of communication that had not been possible before.

In the book, *A Woman's Guide to Successful Negotiating,* Lee and Jessica Miller provide an excellent method of Convince, Collaborate and Create Your Way to Agreement. They say that "Convince is the art of persuasion and is broken down into three basic elements: listening, questioning and delivering your message." The next Characteristic, Empathy is a critical component in developing this ability.

CHAPTER 14

Characteristic 9—Empathy

Feelings, Feelings, Feelings

Empathy is described as: "The action of understanding, being aware of, being sensitive to, and vicariously experiencing the feelings, thoughts, and experience of another of either the past or present without having the feelings, thoughts, and experience fully communicated in an objectively explicit manner; also: the capacity for this."

Talk, Talk, Talk—Conversations!

In her book *Talking from 9 to 5,* Deborah Tannen says that "Conversation is a ritual." We don't think of the literal meaning of the words we say because we say the things that seem like the right thing to say at the time. However, people vary on how they use these rituals, and when a person doesn't recognize the ritual in the first place, they take the spoken words "literally." She goes on to say that differences aren't "expected" and we don't recognize that they are a ritual. The problem is exacerbated when "we think we're all speaking the same language." That "language" comes from our own "frame of reference" which means our beliefs and preconceived notions or mindsets . . . everything that makes up our unique individuality and personality. This is formed from our own individual experiences and can be based upon any variety of sources from our own culture, ethnicity, gender, family of origin, education, work experiences, geographic location, etc. The challenge here is that often times we "expect" that other peoples' experiences "mirror" our own and, there may be similarities. However, in many cases the other person's experiences "differ" and their frame of reference is very different from ours.

Listening: "Say What?"

It's been said that human beings have two ears and one mouth because we need to "listen" twice as much as we speak. To develop self-empowerment, effective communication skills are critical and listening is one of the main components in this area. The key is to allow the other person to "speak" first and only then, when you understand their issue, do you respond. The challenge is that as human beings, we are thinking in our "head" what we are going to say in response to them. We need to learn how to "resist that urge" and hear the other person out.

Hearing vs. Listening: There is a difference between hearing and listening. Hearing is a biological or a sensory response that gathers sound waves indiscriminately. Listening is the ability to understand what a person is saying, why and with what emotions lie behind it and responding appropriately. It is interpreting and, simply put; hearing "occurs," but listening is a conscious "choice."

Communicating 101

Active listening means going beyond a literal comprehension to an empathetic understanding of the speaker. It means "putting yourself in the speaker's shoes" and understanding the emotions they are experiencing. This aids in the communication process.

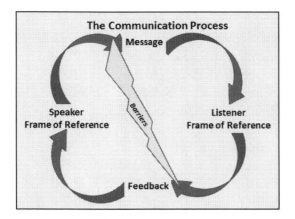

The communication process is an "active" or a transactional process and it works first by the speaker creating, or encoding a message and then sending it to a listener. Various forms of "media" can be used to create and send the message, for example the "speaker" may use:

- Verbal communications and speak directly to the "listener," either in person or via electronic or communications technology, i.e., telephone, voicemail, videophone/conference, webinar, etc.

- "Written or text" media, hard/paper copy, electronic media such as email, blogs, social media, on-line or text communications

- "Non-verbal" communication such as "waving" to get attention or various non-verbal indicators, such as "eye contact," facial expressions, etc.

Upon receiving the message, the listener then decodes it and replies to the speaker's message which is a form of feedback. Seems simple, however, it is not; it is a complex process.

What actually happens is that the speaker is creating or encoding his or her message based on his or her own frame of reference. The frame of reference is based upon their own personal beliefs, values, motives and experiences.

The listener has a frame of reference as well, and while they are decoding or interpreting the speaker's message, they unconsciously interrupt the message by "filtering" the information through it. They then provide feedback to the speaker accordingly. The listener breaks down the information and interprets it based on his or her frame of reference. At times this can act as a "barrier" and cause communications "misfires" because of differences in the frame of reference of both the speaker and the listener because the information both are interpreting back and forth is based upon their own individual frames of reference.

What We Have Here is a Failure to Communicate

An example of how I observed one of these communications "misfires" occurred recently while I was listening to a friend of mine describe a conversation she had with her husband. She had gotten married a few months earlier and was sharing a personal story about an incident that had occurred when she and her then-fiancée were making their honeymoon plans.

As she told the story, she said that when they were planning their honeymoon, she had told her fiancée that she wanted a room overlooking the beach. She went on to say that when he made the reservations he told her that they had a room overlooking the "gulf." However, she "thought" he had said "golf" and was "upset" with the idea that the "view" might be of the golf course. When she realized that he meant "gulf" she said that this was an example of her being a "ditz." In discussing this, I explained to her that what she described was actually a communications "misfire" between a male and a female—that she is an intelligent, talented woman; definitely not a "ditz." We had a good "laugh" over it.

There are two points to be made here, the first being that my friend needed to clarify what her fiancée meant when she though he said "golf." The second being that, as a result of her own "frame of reference," she labeled herself a "ditz," which could lend itself to negative stereotyping. All of which could have been avoided by practicing effective listening skills.

Listening is not a one way street—it's dynamic; and flows both ways. The speaker and the listener are continuously changing roles back and forth. Communication can break down and it often does as a result of the constant transferring of information back and forth, based on the frame of reference. Often the listener does not "hear" the complete message as a result. A way to avoid these communications misfires is to clarify the meaning of the message by learning, developing and employing verbal listening skills.

Listening Skills

Verbal Listening Skills: To help the listener to concentrate on the complete message the speaker is conveying, the listener can employ these verbal listening skills.

- **Interest Statements:** These are verbal indicators given by the listener to signal to the speaker that he/she is listening, such as, "I see," "Go on," etc. During telephone conversations this is really important because the listener cannot see the speaker's body language and is unaware of their non-verbal cues. Also, sometimes during face-to-face conversations, listeners can pretend they are listening by nodding their heads and even making eye contact, but still not understand the message. By responding with interest statements it indicates to the speaker that his or her message is being heard.

- **Empathetic Response:** With these responses the listener acknowledges the speaker's emotions they are experiencing as they are speaking. Typical emotions are anger, frustration, joy etc. Empathetic responses indicate to the speaker that, not only that you are listening, but also that you understand *what they're going through and how they are feeling about it.* For example, if a colleague at work says: "I'm exhausted from working all this overtime every day. I have so much work to do; I can't get it all done . . . and they keep giving me more! I don't know what to do! I just can't handle it anymore." An empathetic response might be to respond by saying something along the lines of: "Gee, you sound like you're feeling really stressed out and overwhelmed. You're unable to finish all the work you're being given even though you're putting in all this overtime." Focus on the emotions you hear the person expressing along with his or her body language, i.e., their demeanor, gestures, tone of voice, eye contact, etc. Acknowledge the situation at hand, as well as the emotions they are feeling. Eliminate any "judgment" of the person or the situation and concentrate solely on the emotions and the circumstances.

- **Ask Clarifying Questions:** The listener asks clarifying questions to help understand exactly what the speaker said, why they said it and what they meant by it. They are used to probe for additional information. For example, in the previous situation with the colleague described above a clarifying question might be: What project are you working on that is making you work all this overtime? Or, that's an awful lot of work, where is it all coming from? Who is giving it to you?

- **Confirm Understanding:** By confirming understanding, the listener verifies that he or she understands what the speaker has said and why he or she said it. The listener can respond by asking a question, such as, "So do you mean the HR Department is assigning all this work?" Or he or she could make a simple statement such as: "So what you're saying is the HR Department is giving you all this work in preparation for the new benefits packages that are going into effect next month." This provides the speaker with acknowledgement that the listener has heard what they said and understands the feelings and emotions they were experiencing.

Learning these listening skills are critical to self-empowerment. They are not easy to master and you may need to take advantage of additional training or education on the topic. However, the benefits of being a good listener far outweigh the investment.

Go Team!

Empathy is a critical component for anyone who is leading a team or is a member of a team. For people to work effectively together towards the attainment of common goals, all team members need to be able to communicate effectively with one another.

Self-empowerment as a team leader or member comes from fostering teamwork by drawing upon the unique and diverse talents of all team members. This is accomplished by asserting themselves, managing conflicts, (which are inevitable when diverse people work together), and listening to other peoples' concerns; which may be conflicting with their own. The next chapter covers the characteristics effective leaders or team members use when collaborating effectively; sharing ideas and concepts and developing mutual strategies and/or solutions to the everyday challenges and problems as they arise.

CHAPTER 15

Characteristic 10—Teamwork

Synergy = Teamwork

Self-empowerment is critical when leading a team or being a member of a team, because it involves bringing together diverse members of a group and getting them to work together to create "synergy" which is the highest level of energy the group can produce. Synergy comes from the Greek word, "synergos," which means "working together." Synergy cannot be "manufactured," but rather it "emerges" as combined "energies" of the team members combine and come together towards the accomplishment of the task at hand. A group of eight to ten people working together can produce much more than eight to ten people working alone.

In my career I have had the privilege of being a member of some great teams. The one that stands out was when I was a part of the learning and education organization of a large corporation. The leader of this organization believed in teamwork and understood what was needed for a team to function effectively; especially by valuing the team members, building relationships and clear, honest communications.

We Just Can't Find Good People Anymore!

Over the years of consulting, training and coaching, the complaints I hear the most from leaders, managers and business people is the difficulty they have motivating and communicating with their team members. They are unable to understand why their team members are "not motivated." They can't get their team members to work together . . . and there's always those "difficult, problem people" who just don't "get it."

Though they mean well, what many of these leaders, managers and business people fail to understand is that not all people share the same motivational drives. As the "Heart Model" illustrates in the earlier section of the model related to "character" and "values," each team member has his or her own "passion," or "fire burning within" them.

I Can't Figure Out How to Motivate Them!

As a leader, I know what motivates me; what I'm passionate about and the tendency is to think that the members of my team will be motivated by the same thing. Nothing could be farther from the truth. The people who share my motivational drive or interests may do well; and we may even think of them as our "stars." But are they really? Are we unknowingly ignoring a "goldmine" of "untapped talent" by not understanding what motivational drives lie dormant within the remaining members of the team? To be an effective team leader, manager or coach, the leader or manager needs to understand what motivates the individual members of the team. It could be any number of varying motivators, such as: achievement, balance, autonomy, job security, power or interpersonal relationships.

> *"Effective Leaders understand*
> *what motivates the individual members*
> *of the team."*

Self-empowered leaders take on the responsibility of getting to know what motivates the members of the team and focus on that when communicating with their team members. They learn to utilize the previously discussed characteristics of collaboration and empathy to communicate in a way that will "speak" to the personal motivational drives of each of their individual team members.

Different Strokes for Different Folks

For example, a team member whose primary motivational drive is "balance" of work and his or her personal life may not be motivated to work on a project that would require them to travel and be away from home for extended periods of time; and it wouldn't matter to them that it was an excellent opportunity for their career or if there were monetary rewards involved. A project such as this might be a better "motivator" for someone whose primary "drive" was that of "achievement," "autonomy" or possibly "power;" depending on the type of project and the type of prestige, compensation or decision-making authority that was involved.

Once a leader exhibits these characteristics, utilizing both collaboration and empathy, they are in a position to tap into the endless possibilities of leading effective teams. A self-empowered leader creates the environment for synergy to emerge.

Why Are We Meeting?

A self-empowered leader needs to be aware of what tasks require the utilization of the team and which ones would be better assigned to individual team members. A good place to start is to understand the purposes of teamwork. The following chart lists the purposes of teamwork. This can be invaluable when working with workgroups and teams. If the task at hand does not appear below, it would be better assigned to an individual and not involve the assembling of the team.

Purposes of Teamwork
Set goals or priorities
Analyze or allocate the way work is performed according to team members' roles and responsibilities
Examine the way the team is working, its processes, such as norms, decision making, communications and so forth
Examine relationships among the team members
Beckhard (1972)

"Welcome to the "Team!"

The next point that is critical for a self-empowered leader to understand is what criteria constitute an effective team.

Criteria for an Effective Team
Understanding, mutual agreement and identification with respect to primary task
Open communication
Mutual trust
Mutual support
Management of human differences
Selective use of the team
Appropriate member skills
Leadership
McGregor, 1967

It is important to concentrate on the third bullet here regarding "Trust." Trust: "I know that you will not—deliberately or accidentally, consciously or unconsciously—

take unfair advantage of me. I can put my situation at the moment, my status and self-esteem in this group, our relationship, my job, my career, even my life in your hands with complete confidence." (McGregor 1967) Of all of these, trust is the most important. A self-empowered leader knows that if a team is to be effective, there must be high levels of trust starting with the leader and amongst all team members.

Stages of Group Development

In 1965 Bruce Wayne Tuckman, Professor Emeritus of Educational Psychology at Ohio State University, developed a theory called "Tuckman's Stages of Group Development." According to Tuckman's theory, all groups or "teams" progress through these stages. Tuckman's original model consisted of four stages: Forming, Storming, Norming and Performing. Later, in 1977, he added a fifth stage; Adjourning.

Tuckman's Model

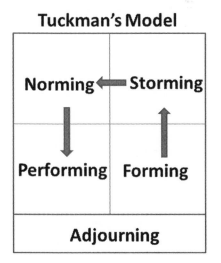

Stage 1: Forming:

This is at the beginning of the team formation process; a new group has just been formed and the new team members are just coming together and getting to know one another. Basically what's happening at this stage is where they are trying to figure out what they're going to do; who's going to do what, etc. At this point they are highly dependent upon the leader for direction and clarity. The leader needs to provide clear objectives and goals as well as be prepared to answer many questions related to the various aspects of expectations such as policies, procedures, etc.

Stage 2: Storming:

As the group moves out of the Forming stage and into this stage, Storming, the team members may begin to experience friction or conflicts with one another. They may resist the directions of the leader as individual personalities begin to arise within the group. Power struggles can, and often do occur between team members and/or the leader. Factions and cliques may develop as individuals vie for status, allegiances and/or control within the group. This can be a very emotional and uncomfortable process.

The Storming Stage is very important in the development of the group and, if the Storming stage is not handled appropriately, the team runs the risk of becoming "dysfunctional" during the course of the project. Many leaders mistakenly think that it "shouldn't be happening" or that "something is 'wrong' (either with the people or themselves"), and thereby try to "sweep it under the rug," attempting to avoid the issues in the hopes that they will "work themselves out." In "denial" of the problems they "move on," however, the problem does not go away, but rather goes "underground" to arise later . . . oftentimes as "problems" during implementation.

Rather than avoid the issues, during this stage the leader needs to address and resolve them. To do this he or she needs to facilitate the group processes and employ effective communications skills such as listening, assertiveness, conflict management and negotiating to move the group to an effective transition into the next stage.

Stage 3: Norming:

As the leader facilitates the Storming stage and begins the processes of resolving the issues identified there, the team transitions into the next stage which is Norming. In Norming, individual roles begin to become more clearly defined. Consensus and agreement begin to occur between individual team members and they begin to cooperate with one another. Commitments are created towards the attainment of mutual goals. A sense of unity emerges and the team members begin to socialize and even have "fun" together. The leader is highly respected. His or her main function now is to enable the team members to achieve their goals. He or she provides direction, motivation and communications for the team and acts as a facilitator for the group processes.

Stage 4: Performing:

At this stage, the team is at its "peak" levels of energy and performance. This is where, when the pressure is on and the deadlines are close, the team's members all come together, and, even though at times the goal may appear "impossible;" somehow, some way, everything comes together (sometimes seeming like "magic"), and the goal is successfully achieved. This is where synergy occurs. It's hard to describe . . . it must be "experienced." Performing comes as a result of all team members being keenly aware and committed to the vision and strategic nature of the goals. The leader's main role at this stage is delegation, observation and availability as a resource. At this stage the leader "gets out of the way" and lets the team do its work.

Stage 5: Adjourning:

Upon receiving feedback after reviewing the results of over twenty studies he performed after his original publication, Dr. Tuckman decided to add a fifth stage to his model entitled Adjourning. This is the "grieving" process a team experiences once the project is completed and the team may be "disbanded." Team members move on to other assignments and projects. It can be as little as a "good-bye handshake" or "farewell luncheon/dinner." It can also be stressful or even emotional and/or painful . . . particularly if the disbanding of the team was not planned or voluntary.

Additionally, whenever the team experiences any sort of a change, either by the leader or a team member "leaving" or "joining" the team, the entire team reverts back to the "Forming" Stage and begins the process over again.

Self-empowered leaders understand these concepts and have learned to facilitate and guide their team members through them. They know when to "direct," "delegate" and "let go" by providing the team members the autonomy needed to accomplish the goals. They had learned to adapt their behaviors to assess each situation as it occurs and to respond in the manner which is best suited for the occasion.

CHAPTER 16

Resiliency Wheel

All these characteristics and skills are overlaid into the Resiliency Wheel and are a critical part of the development of self-empowerment. They are at the center of the wheel and function as the "spokes" that support the entire wheel. The outer part of the wheel; or "where the rubber meets the road" represents behaviors needed to engage in to develop and maintain self-empowerment; scout, educate, build allegiances and grow.

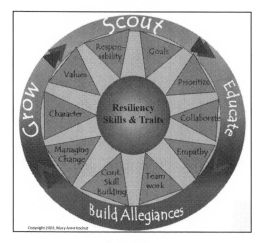

Scout:

This means to continually **"scout"** the environment and be aware what is happening around us. Where are new opportunities? What is happening in society? Where is the culture going? What are some of the things that are happening in our target market? What is affecting our business? We are somewhat like the "surfer" who is always looking over his or her shoulder waiting for the next wave.

Educate:

As a result of "scouting" certain areas may be identified in which **"education"** is needed to keep up with changes in society or technology; new skills to be learned, either personal, interpersonal or technological. For example, in the last ten years the new cars being manufactured no longer have cassette tape players in them. If cassette tapes

125

were a part of your business, you had to transition to CD's or on-line downloading procedures. As a result you may need additional training on how to use the new technology or even return to school to get additional certifications as they relate to the changes occurring in your industry or target market.

Build Allegiances

This is the continued networking; or fellowship with other people. In her book, *The Secrets of Savvy Networking,* Susan Roane says, that "Networking is a reciprocal process, an *exchange* of ideas, leads and suggestions that support both our professional and our personal lives. There is also a spirit of sharing that transcends the information shared. The best networkers reflect that spirit with a genuine joy in their 'giving.'" She goes on to say that, "Being a good networker also means being a **visionary**—having the ability to see the larger picture of the future. We do things for people for no apparent reason or immediate return. 'What goes around comes around' is a tenet of networking and of life." She continues by saying that in order for networking to work, both in a professional and personal nature, it "must reflect certain values. To successfully do business via our contact base requires several current yet old-fashioned qualities, including a solid sense of ethics and a great degree of integrity. Current business literature has catapulted ethics, integrity and honesty back into the limelight."

This is accomplished by reaching out and getting to know people. Get involved by joining professional, business and networking groups . . . do volunteer and pro-bono work. Nurture those relationships that you make. In reality networking is about making contacts and helping other people connect and make additional contacts as well. One of my favorite motivational speakers of all time is the late Zig Ziglar who is known for the quote: "You can get everything in life you want if you will just help enough other people get what they want." This quote is the foundation of networking. While there are no guarantees, and it may not always balance out evenly as in "quid pro quo;" building a strong network and helping other people build theirs as well will strengthen your reputation with your connections in your network. As the old saying goes . . . "It's not what you know, but it's who you know."

Here are some suggestions for successful, effective networking:

- Show up consistently
- Listen for what others need
- Give first
- Ask for what you need
- Meet one-on-one for deeper understanding
- Do what you say you are going to do

Grow

This means that we are always open to additional growth and development; professionally, personally and also spiritually. One of my favorite quotes for many years is by Ray Kroc, who founded the McDonalds franchises. He said: "As long as you're green, you're growing. As soon as you're ripe, you start to rot." I heard this quote very early in my career and it has stayed with me all these years. Whenever I would find myself starting to get too "comfortable" in any situation, I'd remind myself that no matter how much I know; if I'm going to succeed in developing self-empowerment, I need to be open to new growth. I need to continuously be open to growth and developing myself to continue growing in self-empowerment; and it's the same for all of us.

The characteristics of empowerment; the skills and traits that make up the Resiliency Hourglass Model support all of these behaviors. For us to develop self-empowerment we need to learn and exhibit all of these skills and behaviors.

At first, this can seem extremely overwhelming, and almost impossible. However, once we begin to put these skills and characteristics into practice, after time they become part of our routine and then become simpler.

CHAPTER 17

Summary

Self-empowered women leaders know and understand this and understand how critical continuous learning is to their role as leaders and that everyone—team members, colleagues, clients, etc., are learning together and from one another.

Interdependence

All of these characteristics of self-empowerment for women function interdependently of each other. Self-empowerment comes with the knowledge of oneself and recognizing that, while others may be projecting negative stereotypes onto them based on their own personal prejudices, when a woman "empowers" herself, she does not have to react or even pay attention to them. She can successfully move forward towards the accomplishment of her goals.

Just like when all the sand flows through to the bottom portion of thee hourglass vessel, the hourglass is then shaken up and turned upside down again, and, just like in real life, the transformation process starts over again.

Self-empowerment is a simple, though complex process. In all reality, however, it is really common sense, but more of an organized common-sense approach to the process. However, the implementation is not an easy process. But, like anything worth working for, the rewards in the end can be great . . . greater satisfaction and greater accomplishments as we become "unstoppable" in achieving our goals!

REFERENCES

Allen, David, *Getting Things Done: The Art of Stress-Free Productivity*, The Penguin Group, New York, NY, 2001

Carr-Ruffino, Norma, *The Promotable Woman: 10 Essential Skills for the New Millennium*, Book-mart Press, USA

Covey, Stephen R., *The 7 Habits of Highly Effective People*, Simon and Schuster, New York, NY, 1989

Daily Beast (The), 3/8/13, "Sheryl Sandberg Defends Marissa Mayer Slams critics of the Yahoo CEO's telecommuting ban." http://www.thedailybeast.com/cheats/2013/03/08/sheryl-sandberg-defends-marissa-mayer.html, The Newsweek/Daily Beast Company LLC, http://www.thedailybeast.com/,2013

Forbes Magazine 10/24/11, "The 10 Worst Stereotypes About Powerful Women," http://www.forbes.com/sites/jennagoudreau/2011/10/24/worst-stereotypes-powerful-women-christine-lagarde-hillary-clinton

Harragan, Betty Hehan, *Games Mother Never Taught You: Corporate Gamesmanship for Women*, Warner Books, Inc., New York, NY, 1977

Helgesen, Sally, *The Female Advantage: Women's Ways of Leadership*, Doubleday, New York, NY, 1990

Jamison, Kaleel; Reddy, W. Brendan, *Team Building: Blueprints for Productivity and Satisfaction*, NTL Institute for Applied Behavioral Science, Alexandria, VA and University Associates, San Diego, CA, 1988

Jensen, Bill, *Simplicity: The New Competitive Advantage*, Perseus Books, Cambridge, MA, What Is Your Life's Work?, HarperCollins, Inc., New York, NY, 2005

Ray Kroc, http://www.brainyquote.com/quotes/quotes/r/raykroc130750.html#RA9ui4oZABOD1sSu.99

Kubler-Ross, Elizabeth, *On Death and Dying*, Macmillan Publishing Company, New York, NY, 1969

Lewin, Kurt Zadek (September 9, 1890—February 12, 1947), http://en.wikipedia.org/wiki/Kurt_Lewin

Miller, Lee E. and Miller, Jessica, *A Woman's Guide to Successful Negotiating*, McGraw-Hill, New York, NY, 2002

Mintzberg, Henry, *The Nature of Managerial Work*, Harper and Row, NY, 1973

Morrison, Ann M., White, Randall P., Van Velsor, Ellen. *Breaking the Glass Ceiling*, Addison-Wesley, Reading, MA, 1987, 1992.

Managing People and Performance, AT&T Management Education and Training, Somerset, NJ, 1988

Merriam-Webster, http://www.merriam-webster.com/

Roane, Susan, *The Secrets of Savvy Networking: How to Make the Best Connections—for Business and Personal Success*, Warner Books, New York, NY, 1993

Smith, M. K., Bruce W. Tuckman—forming, storming, norming and performing in groups, the encyclopedia of informal education, www.infed.org/thinkers/tuckman.htm, (2005)

Smith, Manuel J., *When I Say No, I Feel Guilty*, Bantam Books, New York, NY, 1975

Spiers, Elizabeth, "Beware of broken glass: the media's double standard for women at the top," http://www.theverge.com/2013/3/6/4070338/beware-of-broken-glass-the-medias-double-standard-for-women-at-the-top, http://www.theverge.com/, 2013

Tannen, Deborah, Ph.D., *Talking from 9 to 5*, William Morrow and Company, Inc., New York, NY, 1994

Thomas, Kenneth W. and Kilmann, Ralph H., Thomas-Kilmann Conflict Mode Instrument, Xicom, Tuxedo NY, 1974, CPP, Inc. Mountain View, CA, 1999

Wilkinson, Bruce *The Dream Giver*, Multnomah Publishers, Sisters, OR, 2003

Young, Valerie, Ed.D, *The Secret Thoughts of Successful Women*, Crown Publishing, New York, NY, 2011

Ziglar, Zig, http://en.wikiquote.org/wiki/Zig_Ziglar, Secrets of Closing Sale (1984the)

ABOUT THE AUTHOR

Mary Anne Kochut is an author, motivational speaker, coach, trainer and organization/management development professional who is skilled in group dynamics, consultation and facilitation. She is Managing Director of Champions for Success, a consulting company that specializes in the areas of leadership, communications, change management, executive coaching and career transition.

As someone who has always had a keen and sincere interest in inspiring people to excel, Mary Anne's personal motto is "committed to the extraordinary." As a result, she remains "in touch" with the most current and provocative issues relative to American business today. She is a determined individual and is committed to inspiring people to live their dreams.

Power vs. Perception: Ten Characteristics of Self-Empowerment for Women is an example of how she has approached and overcome the many challenges she's faced in her personal life and career. She is an engaging and energetic speaker who inspires her audiences through her own personal experiences combined with her commitment to excellence and professional expertise.

Mary Anne is an Adjunct Professor at Passaic County Community College, Paterson NJ, Essex County College, Newark, NJ and Pillar College, Newark, NJ. She holds a Master's of Science Degree in Organization Development from the American University/National Training Laboratories program in Washington, DC. Additionally, she holds the National Training Laboratories Certificate for Organization Development and is qualified to administer the Myers-Briggs Type Indicator.

As a result of more than twenty years of experience in various Fortune 500 Companies, she has a broad background in the area of organization development consulting and training. Her experience ranges from resource development and evaluation to program development and delivery.

She has also been an Adjunct Professor of Management at Fairleigh Dickinson University and has executive experience from the Executive Branch of Government as a Member of the Borough Council for the Borough of South Plainfield, New Jersey.

To contact Mary Anne or inquire about having her speak at your organization, visit www.championsforsuccess.net or email mary@championsforsuccess.net.

Made in the USA
Middletown, DE
05 December 2018